Understanding Testing in Occupational Licensing

Establishing Links Between Principles of Measurement and Practices of Licensing

Jim C. Fortune
and Associates

Understanding Testing in Occupational Licensing

Jossey-Bass Publishers
San Francisco • Washington • London • 1985

UNDERSTANDING TESTING IN OCCUPATIONAL LICENSING
Establishing Links Between Principles of Measurement and Practices of Licensing
by Jim C. Fortune and Associates

433 California Street
San Francisco, California 94104
&
Jossey-Bass Limited
28 Banner Street
London EC1Y 8QE

Library of Congress Cataloging in Publication Data

Fortune, Jim C. (date)
Understanding testing in occupational licensing.

(The Jossey-Bass social and behavioral science series) (The Jossey-Bass higher education series)
Includes bibliographies and index.
1. United States—Occupations—Licenses—Addresses, essays, lectures. 2. United States—Occupations—Licenses—Examinations, questions, etc.—Addresses, essays, lectures. 3. Professions—Licenses—United States—Addresses, essays, lectures. 4. Professions—Licenses—United States—Examinations, questions, etc.—Addresses, essays, lectures. I. Title. II. Series. III. Series: Jossey-Bass higher education series.
HD3630.U7F67 1985 353.0082'43 84-43026
ISBN 0-87589-644-8 (alk. paper)

Manufactured in the United States of America

The paper in this book meets the guidelines for permanence and durability of the Committee on Production Guidelines for Book Longevity of the Council on Library Resources.

JACKET DESIGN BY WILLI BAUM

FIRST EDITION

Code 8509

The Jossey-Bass
Social and Behavioral Science Series

Consulting Editor,
Testing and Measurement

Jayjia Hsia
Educational Testing Service

Preface

Licensing is the act of authorizing a person to do something that is regulated by law to protect public health and safety. Licenses are issued by state boards and federal commissions to candidates who have established evidence of their qualifications, usually by successfully completing an examination process. Licensing is enacted to assure the qualification of new practitioners and to discourage incompetent and unscrupulous practice of the occupation.

From its initiation in the late 1800s until the mid 1900s, licensing was practiced in the United States with little visibility. Since the mid 1900s licensing legislation has proliferated because of technological advances, occupational specialization, and the desire of occupational groups to limit the supply of practitioners and to enjoy the prestige afforded to regulated occupations. Danger to the public and potential ecological contamination have resulted in licensing currently being practiced in real estate, pharmacy, electronics, nuclear-related occupations, banking, maritime engineering, nursing, construction trades, and many other technical vocations offering service to the public. These additional occupations represent a change from the traditionally licensed professions in medicine and law where the public threat is more obvious.

With the proliferation has come increased visibility, due in part to a depressed economy, civil rights, and employment concerns. This visibility is manifested in the number of consulting contracts for technical assistance that have been let by licensing agencies since 1982. Almost all these contracts involve assistance in measurement and data management, reflecting a frequent deficiency in licensing agency staffing.

This book is designed for a wide range of professionals for whom licensing exists, for personnel of state and federal agencies involved in occupational licensing, and for measurement specialists concerned with the tests used in much licensing. It gives professionals a basic understanding of the principles and practices involved in the development, operation and maintenance of a licensing system in regard to measurement. The book's content provides (1) an overview of the history, variations, and effects of licensing; (2) an understanding of the measurement principles, data management requirements, and component relationships essential to a licensing system; (3) familiarity with legal issues and precedents involved in licensing; and (4) acquaintance with the development or operation of two licensing systems, one at the national level and one at the state level. It is expected that this book will also introduce a new and growing area of application to the professionals and researchers in measurement.

Along with providing practical information to people who need to develop licensing programs, this book has been organized with two additional objectives in mind. The first is to facilitate communication between agency personnel and measurement professionals. To accomplish this, the measurement principles discussed in the chapters are presented in as nontechnical a manner as possible in order to maximize their usefulness to a large audience, regardless of readers' prior knowledge of measurement techniques. The second objective is to invite members of the measurement community to become involved with problems associated with the examination process in licensing. Hence, the content is focused on occupational testing for licensing. Contributors to this book have been selected because of their prior experience with licensing.

Since occupational licensing is a developing field, several major issues remain unresolved, most of them having to do with measurement. Unresolved issues include what types of evidence are appropriate for test validation, what evidence of reliability is required, and what methods of developing "cutscores" are appropriate. No attempt has made been to extract professional disagreements on such issues from the chapters in this book. The preservation of each author's point of view is an imperative of science and a reflection of the current state of the art.

Overview of the Contents

Understanding Testing in Occupational Licensing contains ten chapters whose common theme is the relationship of measurement to the practice of occupational licensing. Each chapter has been designed to address some part of this relationship and therefore further the description. Since the chapters were developed with different themes and by individuals with expertise in both measurement and occupational licensing, redundancies in the book serve to identify areas of agreement.

Given the disparate opinions and experiences of the contributors to *Understanding Testing in Occupational Licensing,* the description of the appropriate practice of measurement in licensing that they have generated is amazingly consistent. Occupational licensing's major function is to safeguard public health, safety, and welfare. It is a practice that will command increasing attention from measurement specialists in the future as it enjoys an enlarged role in our society. Licensing also has ancillary functions, such as increasing the prestige of the occupations and limiting access to them.

The first chapter, "Overview of Professional and Occupational Licensing," by Benjamin Shimberg, establishes the frame of reference for the rest of the book, presents a brief overview of the background and history of occupational licensing in this country, and provides a knowledgeable discussion of the issues involved in the practice.

Richard L. Burns, in the second chapter, "Guidelines for Developing and Using Licensure Tests," presents a thorough description of the activities involved in developing the primary evidence of qualification used in the licensing process. His questions, which need to be asked by users of an occupational test, represent a first step toward the application of measurement principles in licensing testing.

The third chapter, "Definitions and Strategies for Validating Licensure Examinations," by Michael T. Kane, gives an accurate and clear discussion of the validating issues involved in testing for occupational licensing. The chapter concludes with a discussion of an eclectic approach to establishing the validity of licensure test interpretations.

In Chapter Four, "Determining Reliability and Validity of Licensure Examinations," James C. Impara and Howard W. Stoker discuss the utility of different forms of the psychometric concepts of reliability and validity for interpreting tests associated with licensing. The chapter is written from a measurement perspective and is directed toward measurement professionals more than agency personnel.

"Legal Issues in Licensing," by Virginia C. Vertiz, reviews the precedents established by judicial hearings concerning occupational licensing. This chapter shows that the practice of licensing derives from the Constitution but that the responsibility for licensing has been allocated primarily to the states. Among the several legal issues addressed in this chapter is the problem of variations in licensing requirements from one state to another for a given occupation. The author discusses the differences in court precedents between tests used in licensure and tests used in employment selection.

Chapter Six, "Validation as a Formative Process: Developing Licensure Examinations for Nuclear Power Plant Operators," by David J. Bowering, Michael T. Wood, and myself, describes an ongoing validation study of the testing program for an occupational licensing system operated at the federal level, with test development work being done through government contracts. In addition to detailing a content validation strategy, the case study illustrates the interaction between politics and measurement methodology.

In the seventh chapter, "Developing and Implementing a State Licensing System," Theodore R. Cromack and Charles S. Coit describe the development of a licensing test and examination maintenance system by a local group for a state-level licensing program. The local group undertook the project because their confidence in national tests that had been used in licensure for the occupation had eroded. This case study illustrates the interaction between local occupational specialists and measurement methodologists.

"Army Programs for Certifying Skills," Chapter Eight, was written by Linda J. Schultz-Shiner and Rebecca L. Oxford-Carpenter, both of the Army Research Institute, to describe skills certification programs in one branch of the military, a practice similar to occupation licensing. The authors describe these programs and the reciprocity agreements that make them an alternative to occupational licensing.

The ninth chapter, "A Systems Approach to Studying Licensing," by Stephanie R. Blecharczyk and myself, provides a conceptual framework for the analysis of occupational licensing as a generic process. In this chapter, we describe the components and requirements of the system.

In Chapter Ten, "Developments and Trends in Licensing and Licensure Examinations," Robert L. Linn argues that public scrutiny of occupational licensing systems should—and probably will—increase in the future. He believes that this scrutiny will surpass that which is currently provided through the "sunset laws" and that expertise in measurement will be needed by those who study and attempt to improve existing systems. Linn also predicts that computers will be a major influence in changing and improving the licensing testing process.

My interest in and involvement with occupational licensing over the past several years is manifested in this volume. I believe that readers will find it useful as well as informative, and I hope that this book will help clarify the testing issues involved in licensing, contribute to the improvement of testing for licensing, and promote increased involvement of measurement professionals in the development process.

Acknowledgments

Linda J. Schultz-Shiner deserves special acknowledgement for work as assistant editor. Her review of the text and her insightful comments were extremely valuable. I also wish to express gratitude to James C. Impara, a colleague, who provided excellent feedback and who devoted extra time and effort to helping me find references and resolve editorial questions.

Blacksburg, Virginia
January 1985

Jim C. Fortune

Contents

The Authors

Jim C. Fortune is professor of educational research and evaluation at Virginia Polytechnic Institute and State University. He received his B.A. degree (1956) from Southwestern College at Memphis in mathematics, his M.A. degree (1959) from Memphis State University in education, and his Ed.D. degree (1965) from Stanford University in education.

Fortune's research activities have focused on the development of evaluation methodology, the evaluation of federal programs, the study of teaching, and the secondary analysis of extant data bases. Also, he has taught research and evaluation methods and measurement and applied statistics and has advised candidates for the doctorate in education.

Prior to joining the faculty at Virginia Tech, Fortune served on the faculties of Memphis State University and the University of Massachusetts and on the staff of the Educational Testing Service.

Stephanie R. Blecharczyk is associate professor of education, Keene State College, Keene, New Hampshire.

David J. Bowering is division vice-president, Science Management Corporation, Washington, D.C.

Richard L. Burns is vice-president, Center for Occupational and Professional Assessment, Educational Testing Service, Princeton, New Jersey.

Charles S. Coit is director, Center for Real Estate Education, University of Southern Maine, Portland.

Theodore R. Cromack is project director of the Commodity Donation Demonstration Study at Virginia Polytechnic Institute and State University, Washington, D.C.

James C. Impara is associate professor of educational research and evaluation, Virginia Polytechnic Institute and State University, Blacksburg, Virginia.

Michael T. Kane is with the Research Division of the American College Testing Program, Iowa City, Iowa.

Robert L. Linn is professor at the University of Illinois at Urbana-Champaign.

Rebecca L. Oxford-Carpenter is a research psychologist, U.S. Army Research Institute for the Behavioral and Social Sciences, Alexandria, Virginia.

Benjamin Shimberg is director of special projects, Educational Testing Service, Princeton, New Jersey.

Linda J. Schultz-Shiner is a research psychologist, U.S. Army Research Institute for the Behavioral and Social Sciences, Alexandria, Virginia.

Howard W. Stoker is professor of educational research and evaluation, Virginia Polytechnic Institute and State University, Blacksburg, Virginia.

Virginia C. Vertiz is intercultural relations coordinator at J. E. B. Stuart High School, Fairfax County, Virginia.

Michael T. Wood is senior research scientist at the Battelle Human Affairs Research Centers, Seattle, Washington, and lecturer in business administration, Pacific Lutheran University, Tacoma, Washington.

Understanding Testing in Occupational Licensing

Establishing Links Between Principles of Measurement and Practices of Licensing

1

Overview of Professional and Occupational Licensing

Benjamin Shimberg

When American society was less complex, there was little need for mechanisms to ensure the competence of practitioners in various occupations and professions. People in a community knew which of their neighbors had completed apprenticeships in the skilled trades and were therefore qualified to provide services at a journeyman's or master's level. And because there was less mobility, it was possible for people to form judgments about a variety of service providers—doctors, dentists, lawyers, and undertakers. However, as America shifted from an agricultural to an industrial society and as cities grew, it became increasingly difficult for people to make judgments about who was qualified and who was not. As America entered the twentieth century, the need for some type of credentialing system became evident.

Actually, two types of credentialing evolved. One was licensing, based on law and involving the police power of the state. The other, certification, was a voluntary system carried out primarily by nongovernmental organizations. Unfortunately, the terms are often used interchangeably, causing considerable confusion.

Licensing and Certification

Licensing is a mechanism by which a legislative body determines, for reasons of public health and safety, that individuals may not engage in certain occupations unless they have received formal permission to do so from a licensing board or from a similar government agency. The licensing process is intended to weed out applicants who lack minimum qualifications.

In order to be licensed, applicants usually must meet certain prerequisites, such as completing training in an approved or accredited institution, completing a period of supervised experience, and satisfying a board of their good character. Only after an applicant has met these or other prerequisites is the individual allowed to sit for the licensing examination. The purpose of the examination, which may include both written and performance measures, is to establish independently that the applicant is at least minimally competent to provide services to the public. Because licensing has its basis in law, the police power of the state may be invoked to prevent unlicensed individuals from practicing.

Certification programs frequently have their basis in law, but most such programs are voluntary. As with licensure, the certification agency usually invokes education, training, and experience prerequisites, as well as an examination requirement. Those who meet the standard are entitled to hang out their certificate and present themselves to the public as "certified," thus differentiating themselves from those who are not certified. Thus the major difference between licensing and certification is that licensing prohibits practice by unlicensed individuals, while certification does not. The confusion between the two terms is compounded by historical use of labels that no longer apply. For example, nurses are licensed, but they are still called "registered nurses" because at one time the names of qualified nurses were placed on an official register. Certified public accountants and registered engineers are both licensed.

New terms are constantly coming up. In the life insurance field, agents and brokers are licensed, but those who meet the standards of the American College of Life Underwriters are entitled to use the title Chartered Life Underwriter (CLU). Physicians who meet the standards of various medical specialty (certification) boards are often called Diplomates. Small wonder that the profusion of titles and their indiscriminate use often leaves the public confused.

This chapter will focus primarily on licensing, although many of the observations apply equally to certification.

Growth of Licensure in the United States. Occupational licensing developed in the United States during the latter part of the nineteenth century. Prior to the enactment of licensing laws, anyone could practice medicine and use the title *physician.* Proprietary schools abounded that for a few dollars would "prepare" anyone for a career in medicine. The better-trained doctors were powerless to stop these poorly qualified doctors from practicing, because there was no law defining qualifications. Finally, under the leadership of the American Medical Association, state legislatures began to pass laws that prohibited all comers from practicing medicine or calling themselves physicians unless they had been licensed by the state medical board.

Other professions and occupations followed the lead of medicine, and by the early 1900s a dozen or more occupations had achieved licensed status. Characteristically, the legislation establishing licensing placed responsibility for implementing the law in the hands of boards made up of practitioners in the licensed occupation. This made good sense at the time because legislators recognized that they knew nothing about entry qualifications, examinations, practice standards, or professional ethics. Such matters, they felt, were best left to leaders from the occupational group. Moreover, since the professional associations had pressed for reform, they were perceived by legislators as protectors of the public interest.

Another indication of the legislature's confidence in boards was the high degree of autonomy granted to them. Most boards were freestanding, not attached to any department of government. They were, in fact, accountable only to the legislature. In addition to reviewing qualifications of applicants and giving examinations, boards also had the power to make rules and issue regulations that had the force of law, so long as these were consistent with the basic statute. Boards also had the power to investigate complaints against licensees and to take disciplinary action where appropriate, including suspending or revoking licenses.

The power of boards to regulate occupations was not lost on nonlicensed groups. In addition to bestowing status and recognition on an occupational group, licensure also gave the group a considerable amount of economic power. Through their control of entry requirements and examinations, boards had control over the supply of practitioners. Through their control of practice standards, boards could determine modes of practice. For example, until recently certain boards prohibited practice by their licensees in commercial establishments. Cases in point are dentists and optometrists, who only lately have been able to establish their offices in department stores or shopping malls.

During most of this century, there has been a vast proliferation of licensed occupations. From a handful in the early 1900s, the number of occupations that are subject to regulation by a local, state, or national governmental entity has risen to 800. Accountants, architects, attorneys, barbers, chiropractors, cosmetologists, dental hygienists, dentists, insurance agents, licensed practical nurses, registered nurses, optometrists, osteopaths, pharmacists, physical therapists, physician/surgeons, podiatrists, and real estate agents are licensed in every state. Some occupations, such as nursing home administrators, are licensed in most states. Still others, such as watchmakers, weather modifiers, auctioneers, and occupational therapists, are licensed in only a handful of states.

With the rise of consumerism during the 1960s and 1970s has come a growing skepticism about the need for so much licensing. Critics of licensing have alleged that occupationally dominated licensing boards often serve the interests of the occupational group more than they do those of the consumer. There are clearly benefits and drawbacks to licensure as it presently exists in the United States.

Benefits and Drawbacks of Licensure. There can be little doubt that the public benefits from licensure when a licensing board conscientiously screens applicants and denies licensure to those who are unqualified. However, the public may not benefit when a board imposes unnecessarily high standards on practitioners or sets unrealistically high score requirements for passing licensing exams. Such artificial restrictions on entry have the effect of limiting the number of practitioners. This means that licensed practitioners may be in short supply and thus may be able to charge more for their services than they could if there were a more competitive market.

The public also benefits when boards set high practice standards and insist that practitioners adhere to them. However, this benefit may be illusory unless the boards have both the capability and the will to investigate complaints and to take appropriate disciplinary action against incompetents or those who violate practice standards.

Standards that define appropriate professional conduct and the relationship between professionals and clients can help to protect the public from unethical or dishonest practitioners. Here too, however, some boards have used standards of conduct to impose restrictions on the business practices of licensees. Price advertising and competitive bidding, for example, were characterized as unprofessional and were prohibited by board rules in a number of occupations, such as pharmacy and optometry. The United States Supreme Court decreed in 1976 that prohibitions against price advertising were illegal because they infringed on the First Amendment rights of those who wished to provide consumers with truthful information.

On balance, the benefits of licensure would appear to outweigh the drawbacks. As with any complex social institution, one can always point to instances where a certain group may have abused its powers or used the situation for its own benefit. These tend to be the exception rather than the rule. Most boards seem to have exercised their powers in a responsible manner, seeking to strike a balance between the interests of the public and those of the occupational group.

Trends and Issues

Debate about the social benefits of licensing has led to a re-examination of the need for so much occupational regulation and to efforts to disband boards that may have outlived their usefulness. In several states (notably Minnesota, Virginia, and Michigan), the legislature adopted procedures designed to make it more difficult for new groups to be licensed. Occupations seeking licensed status had to provide evidence that unregulated practice was causing actual harm to the public. They were also required to show why less restrictive types of regulation, such as registration and certification, were not adequate to deal with the problem evidenced. To help legislators evaluate requests for licensure from new groups, the Council of State Governments asked Shimberg and Roederer (1978) to prepare the booklet *Occupational Licensing: Questions a Legislator Should Ask.*

In 1976, the Colorado legislature passed the nation's first *sunset* law. The purpose of the law was to require a systematic review of all government departments and agencies and to eliminate those that were no longer needed or that were not fulfilling their intended purpose. The law specified a review schedule and stipulated that unless an agency was granted a new lease on life by a positive act of the legislature, it would be allowed to "fade away into the sunset"—hence the term sunset legislation.

Thirty-five other states followed Colorado's lead in passing sunset legislation. In nearly all states, regulatory boards and commissions (rather than larger departments) became the focus of sunset reviews.

Those who thought that the sunset process would result in the wholesale abolition of licensing boards have been disappointed. Relatively few regulatory agencies have been abolished. However, many boards seem to have been motivated to put their houses in better order to avoid criticism. Facts brought out during sunset hearings prompted legislators in several states to introduce reforms such as reorganizing the licensing structure to grant greater authority over board activities to a centralized agency.

Perhaps the most significant outcome of the sunset process and of efforts by public interest groups to achieve reform has been the attention focused on licensing as a social institution. A number of public policy questions have come to the fore. These include ensuring continued competence of practitioners, strengthening the disciplinary role of boards, improving testing practices, making boards more accountable, and giving the public a greater voice in board activities.

Ensuring Continued Competence. Although licensing agencies have shown considerable zeal in screening applicants for initial licensure, they have been much less zealous in monitoring practitioners to make sure that they maintain their competence. There is a tradition that once individuals have been licensed, they may retain their credentials for life. Most licensing laws provide that a license may be suspended or revoked only after the licensee has been accorded a formal hearing and has been found to be seriously incompetent, negligent, or otherwise unfit to practice.

Most boards lack the resources for active monitoring of licensees. Instead, they wait for complaints to come in from consumers, other professionals, or other agencies, such as the Federal Drug Enforcement Agency. Such complaints are investigated (to the extent that resources permit), and formal charges are brought when the allegations appear to be well founded. Under this approach a board might be unaware of licensees who fail to provide quality service, whose health is impaired, or who have numerous malpractice suits pending against them.

Professional groups as well as consumers have exhibited concern about licensees who may no longer be fit to practice. In medicine, for example, state associations have established programs designed to identify and rehabilitate impaired physicians. Many professional associations also require evidence of continuing education to retain continued membership.

The National Advisory Commission on Health Manpower in 1967 took note of the problem of medical obsolescence and concluded that "simply making educational opportunities available will not assure their utilization . . . unless sufficient incentives are provided. One way of providing such incentives would be to relicense health professionals periodically on the basis of acceptable programs of continuing education or on the basis of challenge examination" (pp. 41-42).

Since then, numerous proposals have been advanced for relicensure by examination or by some type of peer review process. Many professional groups found such suggestions objectionable, even offensive. Their response was to suggest the imposition of a continuing education requirement as a condition for relicensure. New Mexico was the first state to impose mandatory continuing education for license renewal of physicians. Many other states have imposed similar requirements for various licensees. According to Phillips (1983), optometrists, nursing home administrators, certified public accountants, physicians, pharmacists, and veterinarians are among the professionals most frequently subject to continuing education requirements.

There is considerable difference of opinion as to the efficacy of mandatory continuing education as a method of ensuring the continued competence of professionals. A study by Bertram and Brooks-Bertram (1977) casts considerable doubt on the value of continuing education itself as a method of upgrading medical skills. However, Stein (1981) arrives at a different conclusion.

In the meantime, other methods of maintaining competence levels continue to be explored. Several medical specialty boards have instituted re-examination requirements. One such board, the National Board of Family Practice, requires all certificate holders to undergo a reassessment process (which includes re-examination) if they wish to maintain their certified status.

Thus far, no state has instituted a mandatory reassessment program. Cost is clearly a major deterrent. Moreover, many people believe that increased emphasis on enforcement and some system of random audits of all practitioners would accomplish the same objective at lower cost.

Strengthening the Disciplinary Role of Boards. Licensing boards have been characterized as "toothless tigers" because of their failure to play a more vigorous role in ferreting out incompetent practitioners and in disciplining those who violate the law or board rules. When challenged to defend their failure to pursue a more active enforcement policy, boards often cite lack of adequate resources and laws so weak that successful prosecution of wrongdoers and incompetents is virtually impossible.

While it is true that legislatures have often been niggardly in allocating resources to boards, it is also true that many boards seem to have lacked the will to carry out investigations or to take strong disciplinary action even after charges against a licensee have been sustained. Similarly, they have not pressed legislatures to pass stronger laws relating to their disciplinary powers.

As a result of sunset hearings, which called attention to serious shortcomings in the disciplinary process, many states have taken steps to strengthen enforcement. In addition, there is a growing recognition that boards may need to increase their monitoring role. Accountancy boards in many states have instituted "Positive Enforcement Programs." These involve making spot checks of certain types of audits. When deficiencies are found, the accountant is called in for consultation. The focus of the program is not so much on discipline as on reminding practitioners that they are expected to adhere to certain standards. Ignoring such reminders could result in disciplinary action.

Improving Testing Practices. Board members are usually appointed for their occupational expertise as well as for their political connections. Seldom are their qualifications in the area of examinations considered. In occupations where national examinations are available, a board member's lack of testing expertise may not represent a serious problem. However, where board members are responsible for developing their own examinations, the result can be serious to both the public and applicants.

In a study of licensing boards in eleven states, Shimberg, Esser, and Kruger (1973) found serious shortcomings in many board-developed tests. Few of the tests that they studied were based on an up-to-date job analysis, and rarely was there evidence of a test plan or specifications to govern test content. Many relied on essay and short-answer questions for which even board members could not agree on acceptable answers. Where performance tests were used, test administration conditions were frequently not standardized, explicit rating criteria were not available, and raters were untrained.

Under such conditions, the tests are unlikely to have sufficient reliability or validity to accomplish their intended purpose. Tests of this type are not fair to applicants because passing or failing may depend as much on the examiner as on the candidate's competence. Nor are they fair to the public. If tests fail to measure essential competencies, the public will not be adequately protected against incompetence. If tests are made unnecessarily difficult, the public may have to pay higher prices for services because the supply of practitioners may be artificially restricted.

Fortunately, there seems to have been a substantial improvement in testing practices since the 1970s. Many more boards now utilize national testing programs. While not all such programs are necessarily of high quality, national tests are more likely to meet legal and professional standards than board-generated tests.

In recent years there has been an encouraging development with respect to board-built tests. A number of states—especially those with strong central agencies—have established test consultation units staffed with examination specialists. These professionals work with boards to conduct job analyses, prepare test specifications, conduct training programs for item writers, review and edit items, perform item analyses, and document the content validity of tests. With such assistance, board tests are often as good as or even better than some national exams.

Making Boards More Accountable. We noted earlier that when licensing boards were first established, they had a great deal of autonomy. These boards were usually not attached to any department of state government but reported directly to the legislature. And since legislators lacked the expertise to regulate these professions, they gave the boards broad powers, including the power to examine applicants, to promulgate rules and regulations that had the force of law, and to suspend or revoke licenses within the framework of administrative due process.

While most boards appear to have exercised their powers in a prudent fashion, isolated instances of abuse—often highly publicized—have led to demands for structural reforms. These reforms have usually taken the form of establishing a centralized licensing agency, often with the goal of introducing a system of checks and balances similar to that which prevails elsewhere in government. According to a study by Roederer and Shimberg (1980), thirty-one states have central agencies, while in the other nineteen, boards remain fully autonomous.

It should be noted that the existence of a central agency does not necessarily mean that a board's decision-making powers are seriously restricted. For example, in seven of the states with central agencies, the agency performs primarily housekeeping functions. In eighteen of the states, however, the central agency goes beyond housekeeping. Board budgets, personnel, and records may be subject to some degree of control by the agency. Complaints, investigations, and adjudicatory hearings may be handled by a central staff even where boards continue to make final decisions with respect to disciplinary actions.

In four of the states surveyed, boards do not have final decision-making authority on substantive issues. While the central agency may delegate many functions to boards, certain board actions (rule making, for example) are subject to review by the agency. In two of the states, licensing boards are advisory. In New York, any board action may be overturned by the state Board of Regents. In Illinois, all board actions are subject to review and approval by the director of the licensing agency.

Most professional groups seem to oppose the trend toward centralization. They argue that only independent boards have the expertise to ensure adequate review of professional standards, to develop examinations, and to make judgments in disciplinary cases. They argue that central agencies merely add layers of bureaucracy, increase costs, and usually provide poorer service to consumers. They believe that autonomous boards made up of dedicated professionals are better insulated against political pressure than a politically appointed agency administrator. Moreover, they say, autonomous boards are more accountable because if either licensees or consumers are dissatisfied, they can go directly to the legislature. Under a centralized system, the legislators are more inclined to leave everything to the central agency.

Giving the Public a Greater Voice in Board Activities. When self-regulatory boards were initially created, neither professionals nor legislators appeared to visualize any role for laypersons. After all, what did laymen know about entry qualifications, practice standards, or professional ethics? In recent years, however, consumers have come to recognize that what boards do can affect the cost, quality, and availability of goods and services. They have insisted on a greater voice in the regulatory process.

The idea of placing public members on regulatory boards has gained a high degree of acceptance from trade and professional groups as well as from consumers. Public members are now found on one or more licensing boards in nearly every state. Public members constitute a minority of the membership in all states except California and Hawaii, where they are a majority on many.

There have been few studies of the role that public members play or the nature of their contributions. Shimberg (1982) provides a number of anecdotal reports which indicate that when public members are carefully selected and given appropriate training, they can make useful contributions. A less optimistic picture is provided by Chesney (1981), who found that public members in Michigan give themselves generally low evaluations on "effectiveness," a perception that is shared by professional members on the same boards.

Putting Licensing into Perspective

After more than a half century of uncritical acceptance as a consumer protection device, licensing became a target of consumer and public interest groups who discovered that some boards were using their powers to promote the interests of their own occupational groups. These abuses seem to have been limited to a relatively small number of boards, yet boards in general were tarred with broad-brush allegations of anticompetitive activity, unnecessary restrictions on entry and mobility, and failure to protect the interest of consumers.

In this writer's opinion, such allegations are unfair and unwarranted. In his experience, extending over nearly two decades, he has found that most board members are very conscientious. They devote much time and energy to board affairs, rarely seek any special benefits for themselves, and receive little appreciation for their efforts.

There is no denying that, like most institutions, licensing has its shortcomings. Some of these stem from the way in which board members are selected. By relying almost exclusively on professional associations for nominations, the appointing authority, perhaps unwittingly, creates boards that are quite homogeneous in their thinking and that usually reflect association policies in their decisions. This might be remedied if a greater effort were made to recruit qualified professionals with diverse viewpoints, which could produce a greater interplay of ideas and values in the decision-making process.

Board members also need a more intensive orientation to their duties and responsibilities. They need to understand more clearly the distinction between a board and a professional association. The latter is responsible to its members, the former to the public.

Boards often must function with inadequate staffs and financial resources. Although they have a responsibility to protect the public, they are usually required to operate on the basis of license fees. As a rule these fees are adequate to cover conventional, multiple-choice testing and other administrative expenses, but they are inadequate to ensure thorough investigations and vigorous enforcement. When boards try to do a good job and take action against licensees by revoking their licenses, they often may be forced to cease further enforcement activities because their resources are drained by the costs of resulting litigation and appeals.

Finally, boards must face up to their responsibility to ensure the continued competence of licensees. It is unrealistic, however, to ask boards to consider re-examination, practice audits, or positive enforcement programs without additional financial support. Board members already contribute time worth millions of dollars to the state. We as citizens owe them greater support then they have received in the past. But in return for the privileges and other benefits that go with licensure, the public has the right to demand greater accountability from all licensing boards and to insist that licensees fulfill their responsibilities to the public.

References

Bertram, D. A., and Brooks-Bertram, D. A. "The Evaluation of Continuing Medical Education: A Literature Review." *Health Education Monographs,* 1977, *5* (4), 330-362.

Chesney, J. F. *Report on the Role and Effectiveness of Public Members on Licensing Boards.* Lansing, Michigan: Health Occupations Council, 1981.

National Advisory Commission on Health Manpower. *Report of the National Advisory Commission on Health Manpower.* Vol. 1. Washington, D.C.: U.S. Government Printing Office, 1967.

Phillips, L. E. "Trends in State Relicensure." In M. R. Stern (Ed.), *Power and Conflict in Continuing Professional Education.* Belmont, Calif.: Wadsworth, 1983.

Roederer, D., and Shimberg, B. *Occupational Licensing: Centralizing State Licensure Functions.* Lexington, Kentucky: Council of State Governments, 1980.

Shimberg, B. *Occupational Licensing: A Public Perspective.* Princeton, N.J.: Educational Testing Service, 1982.

Shimberg, B., and Roederer, D. *Occupational Licensing: Questions a Legislator Should Ask.* Lexington, Ky.: Council of State Governments, 1978.

Shimberg, B., Esser, B., and Kruger, D. *Occupational Licensing: Practices and Policies.* Washington, D.C.: Public Affairs Press, 1973.

Stein, L. S. "The Effectiveness of Continuing Medical Education: Eight Research Reports." *Journal of Medical Education,* 1981, *56,* 103-110.

2

Guidelines for Developing and Using Licensure Tests

Richard L. Burns

Almost all occupational licensing includes some type of testing. For that reason, it is important that the basic principles and practices associated with testing—especially as they apply to occupational licensing—be clearly articulated and understood. The purpose of this chapter is to discuss these basic issues.

This discussion will not be highly technical or heavily research-oriented. Rather, it will review testing for occupational licensing in terms of what the nonmeasurement expert, the typical licensing administrator, should know and be alert to. While some use of testing terminology is unavoidable, it will be kept to a minimum and explained wherever used.

The critical issues and approaches important to the licensing administrator will be identified and discussed. Finally, the chapter offers a series of questions suggesting to administrators the critical elements they should raise with the experts who are working with them on the testing component of licensing.

The chapter is organized into six sections, each intended to structure a logical progression through the problems and issues of testing for occupational licensing. The sections are (1) deciding what to test, (2) deciding how to test, (3) developing psychometrically sound tests, (4) ensuring the integrity of the testing process, (5) ensuring sound interpretation and use of test results, and (6) questions a licensing administrator might ask about testing.

Deciding What to Test

The Purpose of the Test. Deciding on the purpose of the test is a critical but too often overlooked first step in deciding what to test. Obviously, the test is to contribute to the licensing process. But in what way and how?

Licensing most often is concerned with protecting the public from practitioners who do not have sufficient knowledge or skills to perform their profession or occupation at an acceptable beginning level without serious risk to the public welfare. It follows, then, that the test used in support of the licensing process should have as its purpose the differentiation between those applicants who have the minimum knowledge and skills and those who do not.

Thus, the purpose should be relatively clear. The test is concerned with minimum knowledge and skills, not with higher-level skills and knowledge. It is concerned with differentiating between those who are likely to do harm to the public and those who are not. Licensing tests are not concerned with identifying those practitioners who are going to be most successful in the occupation. Rather, most states have determined that the examination should help determine that the agent understands the functions and responsibilities of the job in accordance with the law and in conformity with rules and regulations of the licensing agency.

Unfortunately, there are instances in which licensing tests have been used for other purposes. In some cases, standards have been set so high that entry into the profession is restricted, service to the public is therefore restricted, and higher prices result. When this occurs, the purpose of the test and its use have been distorted.

Licensing administrators have often relied on their own judgment and experience or that of educators in deciding what the purpose and content of the examination should be. Too often, this subjective selection of criteria results in tests that reflect what is in the training curriculum, whether or not that is based on what is needed at the entry level to protect the public. A more objective method is normally more desirable.

Job-Relatedness. Given the purpose for licensing tests (to establish evidence of competence to practice at the entry level), it is critical that the tests be job-related. Such a test should include only material directly related to a beginner's performing a particular job. For example, selling skills, while clearly relevant to success in an insurance career, are not relevant for licensing purposes and questions about them would be inappropriate in an examination for insurance agents.

Similarly, information that might be desirable from an academic perspective and that might be included in a training program for an occupation, but which is not critical to doing the job at a beginning level, would also be inappropriate. For example, knowing who discovered various drugs may be considered important by professors in a school of pharmacy and might even provide a pharmacist with interesting conversational material, but such facts have little relevance to licensure. The absence of that knowledge will not affect the pharmacist's ability to dispense drugs effectively and in conformity with the standards of the profession or the laws of the state.

The method increasingly used for establishing the job-relatedness of a licensing examination is a formal job analysis. A job analysis is a systematic method of determining what a practitioner actually does on the job. It provides a way to describe the most important functions and responsibilities of the job and what the entry-level practitioner needs to know and be able to do in order to carry out those responsibilities and functions. The focus is on acceptable performance, not outstanding performance.

Several basic approaches to job analysis are employed. The approaches range from a relatively straightforward use of a committee of job experts, through obtaining critical incidents from job incumbents and supervisors, to obtaining questionnaire results from a large representative sample of job incumbents. The most commonly used approach involves a combination of techniques. (A number of references are listed in the

"Additional Readings" section of this chapter for those interested in more information on the basic approaches.) Basically, whatever the approach taken, the objective is to describe the aspects that are important to performing a job in a satisfactory manner. Test specifications can then be developed based on the findings of the job analysis.

One common approach to job analysis identifies and describes principal job tasks through use of a questionnaire survey. The analysis generally starts with a literature search to provide a knowledge base. Job descriptions, other studies on the job, and any other relevant information are reviewed. On-the-job observations are often made. On the basis of this information, a preliminary job description is assembled. Simultaneously, a panel or committee of experts on the job is identified. The committee usually consists of a mixture of practitioners, supervisors, and trainers or educators for the job. The job analyst works with the committee to develop a more accurate picture of the job. Relying heavily on their knowledge of the job, the job analysts develop a questionnaire that attempts to detail the major functions and responsibilities involved in the job. After agreement from the committee that the result is an accurate picture of the job, the questionnaire is sent out to a large sample of individuals who are functioning in the job and, in some cases, to their supervisors. Respondents are typically asked to rate each task on several different rating scales, such as its importance, the time spent on it, the level of judgment and ability required to perform the task, and whether or not the task is critical for those entering the profession or occupation. The findings of this task inventory are then analyzed, and a report is created that clearly identifies those tasks that are important to be performed by an entry-level licensee.

The results of the job analysis must be documented to be useful and must then be used in the test development process if they are to have an impact.

Test Specifications. Test specifications are the blueprint or plan for the test. In academic settings they usually reflect the curriculum being examined. In testing for licensing they must reflect the job being licensed. Each item in the test should be capable of being linked to tasks identified in the job analysis. This is typically accomplished through a linkage study in which knowledge, skills, and abilities are specifically tied to the test specifications by a committee of experts in the field being tested.

It is important that the linkage process be documented, both to produce a record for future reference and to use in the event of legal challenge. Documentation usually takes the form of a detailed chart or a report showing the relationship between the results of the job analysis and the test specifications.

Constraints. What has just been described is, of course, the ideal arrangement. Sometimes constraints may reduce the degree to which all aspects can be carried out. In some cases, the money for a full-scale job analysis is not available. In others, the populations to be tested are too small to warrant the kind of effort outlined earlier.

When operating under constraints, the licensing authority may choose to shortcut some steps of the process. However the determination is made, someone must define in a defensible manner the purpose of the test and how the test content relates to major entry-level aspects of the job. The risk in not going the more formal route is that a less satisfactory and less appropriate test may result and if legal challenge is brought, it may be more difficult to defend the test.

Legal considerations will be discussed to a limited degree later in this chapter and more fully in Chapter Five. However, the relevant basis for much of what is proposed here is the federal "Uniform Guidelines on Employee Selection Procedures" (Equal Employment Opportunity Commission and others, 1978) and other standards that will be discussed later. The guidelines, a joint statement of the EEOC, the Civil Service Commission, the Department of Labor, and the Department of Justice, concern employment testing; while they make reference to licensing and certification testing, the statute under which they were issued (Title VII of the Civil Rights Act of 1964) has generally been held to be inapplicable to occupational licensing activities of state agencies. In spite of their questionable legal relevance to licensing testing, the guidelines may be called on in legal challenge brought by members of racial, ethnic, and gender subgroups protected by federal employment discrimination law.

Deciding How to Test

In reviewing job analysis results for development of test specifications, it is important to recognize that there may be aspects of the job that cannot be effectively assessed through the use of a written test. In some instances performance measures or simulations may be called for. In others a review of experience may be the most appropriate, cost-effective approach. When determining how to assess, it should be clear that what is to be tested can be measured in a professionally sound and legally defensible manner.

Clearly, determining what testing methodology should be used is directly related to the decision on what to test. The nature of the subject matter, the testing objectives, and the critical elements of the job are directly related to the method of testing. For those occupations in which knowledge and skills can be demonstrated through written tests, one need not consider performance tests or simulations, but when the minimum level of competency requires some type of physical manipulation, such methods may be called for.

The important consideration is that the testing technique must be appropriate to the objective of the testing and to the critical elements of the occupation being tested. With real estate agents, for example, it is reasonable to limit the testing to a paper-and-pencil test of knowledge of real estate principles and practices and relevant national and state laws. For a barber, however, such a test, while undoubtedly a part of the licensing process, would be insufficient to determine whether or not the applicant had the skill to cut hair in a safe and healthy manner. A performance test is one possibility. It may not always be the answer, however. Where the applicants have been trained in an accredited school and have worked under supervision, it may be reasonable to assume that the individual can perform at the entry level, without giving a test to establish that fact. A checkoff procedure could be developed where certified instructors attest to a candidate's ability to perform a given task.

Testing Alternatives. The principal alternatives used in licensing testing are multiple-choice, essay and short answer, oral, simulation, and performance testing. The computer can be the vehicle for all of these, except oral and performance testing. In those cases (as well as with the other alternatives), other kinds of technology, such as an audio- or videotape, slides, videodisks, and so on, can be employed. This section will briefly define each of these basic forms of testing and discuss their strengths and weaknesses. The forms can, of course, be used in combination. Computer applications of particular testing techniques will be treated separately.

Multiple-choice testing consists of a series of questions in which stimulus material is presented in the first part, or *stem,* of the question and is usually followed by four or five numbered or lettered choices. One of these choices, the *key,* is correct and the others, the *distractors,* are incorrect, or in some types of multiple-choice testing, less correct. In some cases a common set of stimulus material, for example, a situation, is presented and a number of questions follow which refer back to that stimulus material. Multiple-choice testing is highly flexible and can be used to test not only for straight recall of factual information but for understanding, application, and integration of knowledge as well. Because each question takes a relatively short time to consider and respond to, a significant number of questions can be presented in a short time period. This flexibility contributes to broad coverage of the domain of knowledge and skills being considered and usually results in a very reliable measure. The multiple-choice format is the most widely used in licensing testing.

Multiple-choice testing can also be used as a kind of simulation test. In what are called *patient-management problems (PMPs)*, a situation is presented, usually a medical or health-related one, followed by a set of options for courses of action that the respondent may take. The results of those actions are initially concealed but can be revealed to the respondent after a choice is made by using a special ink pen applied to a concealed or latent-response choice. This type of item is sometimes referred to as a *latent image item.* In one application of PMPs, all candidates follow the same sequence regardless of the choice of action made. These are referred to as *linear PMPs.* In the other approach, the choices a test-taker makes determine the questions that follow, and the test-taker is routed through the test in terms of the results of the actions he or she takes. These items are *branching PMPs,* and while more difficult to score and create, they are more realistic and appear to have greater validity. In recent years users of linear PMPs have tended to abandon the approach, largely on the grounds that they are too much like a series of independent multiple-choice questions to warrant the extra expense in preparation and scoring. Branching PMPs, however, are even more difficult and expensive to create, print, and score and hence are not widely used. When a computer is used to present PMPs, scoring and other problems can be reduced or eliminated.

The basic characteristic of *essay and short-answer tests* is that the test-taker generates his or her response in written form rather than selecting from alternative answers. In an essay test, the test-taker is expected to provide a coherent and integrated response to what is usually a relatively involved or complex set of stimulus material. In the short-answer form, a word or two or a phrase or sentence is all that is expected.

By definition, essay tests examine writing skills as well as subject-matter knowledge. Unless writing skill is necessary for job performance, the use of such a measure can compound the measurement problem due to the difficulty of distinguishing between the style and correctness of the presentation and the correctness of the response. Failure to recognize and deal effectively with this problem can lead to serious legal problems. Agreeing in advance on acceptable responses and their relationship to minimal standards is also a critical need. The costs and time required for grading essay tests are major considerations in the choice of either essay or short-answer testing. The importance of training graders and following procedures that ensure consistency in applying grading standards further complicates and adds to the cost of essay testing. Where writing skill is an important consideration and where adequate care is taken to deal effectively with the problems identified, essay testing can provide a useful measurement tool. Essay testing is widely used in testing lawyers for admission to state bars.

In *oral tests,* the responses to questions are given orally and are not written down. Usually the stimulus material is presented orally as well, but it may involve pictures, X-rays, graphs, tables, or other visual materials. Oral tests are typically scored by the people who administer them. Although responses can also be audiotaped or videotaped and scored later, this is typically not done for cost reasons. Standardization of presentation, comparability of questions (for security reasons, a large number of different questions are usually used, introducing the problem of differential difficulty), comparable content coverage, and standardization and consistency of grading criteria are major problems with this approach. However, such tests seem highly relevant and appropriate to both the test-taker and the tester and in many occupations can be designed to be highly job-related.

While *performance testing* is frequently used in industry for job selection, it is seldom used for licensing. A major factor is the time and cost involved in administering and grading performance tests, especially when the candidate volume is high. Many cosmetology and barber boards still use performance tests in which candidates cut hair and perform other functions such as permanent waving or hair relaxing. While neither medical or nursing boards use performance tests, dental boards still do so. The candidate is required to find a patient whose teeth are in need of the specific dental procedures called for by the exam. This may involve filling a cavity with an amalgam or making a gold foil cast.

There are a number of critical requirements that must be satisfied by a sound performance test. Directions and administrative conditions must be standardized. Clear and unambiguous standards for grading must be established so that the graders will be able to differentiate between acceptable and unacceptable performance. Training and monitoring the raters is critical to make sure that they are applying standards correctly and consistently. Finally, there is the problem of possible sex bias or racial bias if raters are permitted to have direct contact with candidates. Californian and a number of regional dental examining boards have instituted procedures whereby the raters examine patients (without even seeing the candidate for licensure who did the work) to evaluate how well the tooth has been prepared and how closely the final product meets the standard.

For some types of performance testing, equipment and space availability, practicality, and safety concerns may be serious constraints. It may not be possible to secure the expensive equipment necessary to carry out a proper performance test. *Simulation testing* can often solve this problem by simulating equipment and situations at much lower cost and risk. However, simulations sometimes involve the use of equipment as well, and if the number of applicants is large, this too can be a constraint.

The critical requirements in simulation testing are that the simulation be an accurate sample of the work, that it be sufficiently realistic to substitute for performance in a real situation, and that it be possible to evaluate the results objectively. Simulations are typically used when some types of physical manipulation are involved, and use of a live situation is too expensive, impractical, or dangerous to the individuals or the equipment required. Some simulations, such as those for flight training and evaluation, can be very elaborate and require extensive and expensive equipment. The equipment is, however, reusable, safe, and unlikely to be damaged in the process of testing. The tester must be careful, however, that the simulation replicates critical aspects of the job and not some extraneous factor such as verbal ability. As with essay testing, a critical aspect of simulation testing is defining in advance what will constitute acceptable minimal performance.

Use of the Computer. The computer has for many years played a major role in the scoring and reporting of licensing test results. Recently, however, it has begun to emerge as a significant testing aid. Some tests in standard multiple-choice format are being administered via a computer terminal. Computers are being used to provide job simulations. When they are linked with videodisk players, highly realistic and varied stimulus material can be presented. The principal current problem restricting the widespread use of computers for licensing tests is the cost of computer hardware (not the cost of an individual terminal but the cost of enough to serve the large numbers of candidates involved) and the cost of supervising their use. That computers can materially improve the testing process in a number of significant ways is not an issue. Whether or not they can do so on a wide scale and on an economically viable basis remains to be seen.

Other Constraints and Considerations. In determining what method to employ for licensing tests, a number of constraints and considerations must be considered before making the choice.

Most often, cost is a fundamental constraint. The most economical form of testing large numbers of individuals is, of course, the multiple-choice test. It often is selected for that reason alone, although it also has a number of other advantages. For very small populations, however, it may not be the most economical or even professionally desirable approach.

Time is often a major constraint—for development of a testing instrument, for administration of the test, and for its scoring and reporting. Time is sometimes closely linked to cost, although not always if all three elements of the time involved are considered.

For some types of testing, for example, oral or performance testing, the availability of examiners in sufficient number and quality to conduct or observe and score the tests can be critical constraints. Highly successful practitioners may not be willing to give up time from their practices to participate in the testing process. In some cases, however, oral testing is used not so much because it is the most appropriate or effective but rather for political reasons. Practitioners often enjoy being oral examiners, see it as prestigious, and, because of tradition, believe that the examination process would be incomplete and invalid without the oral testing in which they participate. Belief in the necessity of oral testing sometimes persists in spite of research evidence to the contrary.

Coverage of a wide range of subject matter is often an important consideration for both validity and credibility reasons. Multiple-choice or short-answer approaches can cover quickly and efficiently a broad range of subject matter at different levels of difficulty. Essay, oral, and, in some situations, simulation and performance testing typically cannot cover the same range of content without extensive and often impractical testing time.

Multiple-choice tests lend themselves well to machine scoring at low cost and a high level of accuracy and speed. The other forms of testing can be adapted to machine scoring, but they require that the scorer rather than the test-taker fill out a machine-scorable answer sheet. Essays normally require a fair amount of time for grading, especially if significant numbers of test-takers are involved and multiple readings are required. Grading standards for all but multiple-choice and short-answer tests are often difficult to establish and maintain.

Finally, psychometric considerations that will be discussed later, such as those relating to validity and reliability, must be taken into consideration. Total reliance on a testing technique, such as an oral test, may raise questions about whether or not raters can agree on common standards and apply them consistently. For that reason and others mentioned earlier, multiple-choice testing is often combined with one of the other techniques in order to increase the validity and reliability of the testing process.

Developing Psychometrically Sound Instruments and Procedures

Validity. Validity is commonly defined as evidence that a test is measuring what it claims to be measuring or predicting. Some people feel a test is valid if it seems reasonable or appropriate. This is referred to as *face validity* and carries no real weight professionally or legally. Generally, three components of validity are considered: *criterion-related, content,* and *construct.* A detailed discussion of these concepts appears in Chapter Three.

In recent years some parts of the psychometric community have argued for an integrated theory of test validity in which all three types of validity are considered. Ideally, according to the integrated theory, a test should be developed in a way that assures its content validity. If it is feasible to do so, studies should later be conducted to ascertain whether the test correlates with an appropriate criterion of job performance. Studies can be conducted to find out if the test behaves as one would expect. For example, scores on a test of basic science would be expected to correlate with grades in science courses. If they did not, one might question the meaning of the construct "knowledge of basic science."

In practice, however, emphasis is normally placed on one type of validity. For licensing testing this has been and is likely to continue to be content validity. Unlike the academic admissions test and the employment selection test, the purpose of the licensing test is not to predict success. Aside from this difference in basic purpose from the tests for which criterion-related validity is appropriate, there are significant technological and logistical problems in conducting a criterion-related validity study on a licensing test. First, there is the substantial difficulty, if not impossibility, of adequately defining an appropriate criterion against which to measure the predictive power of a licensing test. The normal measures of success in a licensed profession or occupation, such as number and size of sales or professional recognition, do not relate to the basic purposes of licensing and are therefore not appropriate criteria. Second, the identification and involvement of criterion-related validity study participants normally poses major logistical difficulties in the licensing situation, as opposed to the employment or academic setting. For these reasons criterion-related validity is rarely considered in licensing. Content validity, on the other hand, can be directly demonstrated by relating test content to job content at the entry level and restricting content to those elements which are critical to protection of the public.

Reliability. Reliability is the extent to which the measurement is consistent or accurate when repeated. Do we get essentially the same results when remeasurement occurs? Some error is inevitable with all measurement, whether educational, licensing testing, or the physical testing of materials or phenomena such as temperature. A test that lacks adequate reliability cannot be valid. For example, in spite of the small error inherent in a common yardstick, it is a useful measurement tool. However, if it were made of an elastic material which was off by several inches either way whenever it was used, it would be of little value.

Reliability measures the extent to which errors of measurement influence scores on the test. The reliability of a test can be measured in a variety of ways, as discussed in Chapter Four. Typically, however, indices of reliability focus on the extent of measurement error over the full score range of test scores. A variety of statistical models and formulas exist for reporting reliability information, although most typically a correlation coefficient is used to indicate the degree of reliability. Total test reliabilities (expressed as coefficients) in the high .70s to low .90s are typical and considered to be sound statistical evidence of substantial reliability.

In most employment and educational testing situations, it is considered highly desirable to have adequate reliability across the full range of scores so that one can have confidence in high scores, low scores, and those in the middle range. In licensing testing, the concern is not with those who are clearly qualified (those making high scores) or with those who are clearly not qualified (those making very low scores). The concern is with those just above and just below the passing point. If scores in the "cut score" range are not reliable, some people who are qualified might be denied licensure, while some who are not qualified might be given the license. It is because of the importance attached to these pass-fail decisions that the principal concern for licensing tests is with the reliability around the passing point rather than across the full range. More information on the various approaches to determining reliability at the passing point is given by Subkoviak (1980).

It is important for licensing administrators to recognize that wherever the cut or passing point is set and however good the test, some error will exist in the measurement and in scores. As a result, some individuals will pass who theoretically should not (if perfect validity and reliability were possible) and some who should pass will not. The value of high reliability is to keep those numbers as small as possible. Estimates of the extent of the error can be obtained by referring to the *standard error of measurement,* the extent to which the reported score is likely to be different from an individual's "true score," if we could obtain it, for the total score range.

Test Development. The basic process of developing a test and the care taken in the process to ensure that appropriate procedures are followed and that quality control is stringently exercised are crucial in achieving psychometrically sound tests. Once the purpose of the test has been established and the basis for determining the test content defined (for example, on the basis of job analysis results), test specifications are created.

The test specifications are, in effect, the blueprint or plan for the construction of the test. They normally deal with the test's major content areas, levels of cognition (recall, application, understanding), types of items, and difficulty level. When job analysis results or some other definition of entry-level job requirements are available they will form the basis for the test specifications.

Questions are usually produced by specialists in the specified content areas. The quality and clarity of the questions are usually improved if the question writers are trained and receive critiques of their efforts by persons experienced in test development. Questions should be reviewed by persons other than the question writer for both accuracy and appropriateness of the content and for clarity and accuracy of presentation. This usually involves reviews by experts in other subject matters, editors, and test development experts. Finally, it is critical that the correctness of the answer be established. For multiple-choice tests, this usually is accomplished by obtaining identification of the correct answer from other experts independently and eliminating questions for which complete and ready agreement on the correct answer is not obtained. For nonmultiple-choice tests, review and discussion of acceptable responses, either derived from actual test-takers or constructed by groups of experts, is required to arrive at agreed-upon scoring.

Closer statistical control of the test is possible if items with available performance statistics (because they have been previously used or pretested) are used. Statistical specifications, means and distributions, for example, can be established for item difficulty and relationship to success on the test as a whole. Pretesting of items, that is, trying them out on a sample of test-takers similar to that on which the items will be used operationally, also permits identification of potential problems with the items and their correction prior to actual operational use. When pretesting is not possible, as it may not be for practical, financial, or administrative reasons, an item analysis of the test prior to final scoring can serve a similar purpose of identifying problem items. Rather than changing any troublesome items identified at that stage, however, they would either be omitted or all candidates would be given credit at the time of final scoring.

Finally, tests are assembled to the test specifications from accepted and approved questions and the test is administered. While test quality is determined largely by what goes into the process, that is, adequacy and quality of the job analysis, test specifications, and question development and review, the quality can be affected both during the test's administration and after.

During test administration, strict adherence to standardized and appropriate procedures, such as directions, test conditions, timing, seating, and proctoring to prevent cheating, is critical. Following the administration, a willingness to recognize the fallibility of the process and its participants and to provide procedures to deal with this is essential. With multiple-choice testing, it is relatively easy to determine how well the test as a whole performed and to identify individual questions with problems. This is accomplished by means of an item analysis that shows the difficulty level of each question item and the relationship of each question to the total score. Questions which prove very difficult or which do not produce results comparable to total score (for example, questions on which high-scoring test-takers have not given the correct answer) can be reviewed again for correctness and appropriateness and, if found flawed, corrected through the revision of the scoring keys or eliminated from scoring before final results are reported. Similar, though less rigorous, approaches can be followed for other types of testing.

An evaluation of the effectiveness or quality of the test

should be made after its administration. This is typically done through a test analysis, which gathers relevant information about the quality of the test. It typically includes summary data on question performance, reliability, speededness (whether or not most candidates finish the test in the alloted time), and other factors that may influence test performance. Although test analysis is easier to conduct with multiple-choice tests, some form of test quality review should be made following the administration of any type of test.

Professional and Legal Standards. All testing is regulated, voluntarily and by law, according to various standards. The present principal professional measurement standards are the *Standards for Educational and Psychological Tests* (American Psychological Association, 1974). These standards spell out in some detail what should be done in respect to test development, validity, reliability, and other areas to create tests that are professionally sound. These standards are currently being rewritten by the three professional organizations concerned with testing (American Psychological Association, American Educational Research Association, National Council on Measurement in Education). If approved, they will be issued as the *Joint Technical Standards for Educational and Psychological Testing.* Adoption is not anticipated before late 1984 at the earliest. As presently drafted, the new standards are more extensive and rigorous than the current standards; moreover, unlike the 1974 standards, the proposed *Joint Technical Standards* contain a chapter devoted to licensing and certification testing.

In addition, the National Commission for Health Certifying Agencies (NCHCA) has established a set of standards that must be met by certificating organizations seeking the imprimatur of the NCHCA. These standards include some psychometric criteria but also deal with policy matters such as the independence of the certifying agency from the professional association.

At least one testing firm, Educational Testing Service (ETS), has developed and makes publicly available a set of standards to which it holds itself accountable. These are the *Educational Testing Service Standards on Test Quality and Fairness,* which were adopted by the ETS board of trustees as corporate policy in October 1981. These standards encompass the principal professional standards on testing discussed above, but they go beyond to deal also with matters such as accountability, accuracy, timeliness, confidentiality, and other matters. All ETS testing programs are audited by committees composed of nonprogram ETS staff and outside experts once every three years. In addition, a Trustee Visiting Committee comes to ETS annually to review the process and the results and provides a report to the trustees. Both the Standards and Visiting Committee Report are available from ETS.

The principal legal standards applicable to the occupational licensing activities of state agencies are the Fourteenth Amendment to the United States Constitution and federal civil rights statutes embodying its requirements. Under the Fourteenth Amendment's equal protection clause, agencies are prohibited from discriminating against licensure applicants who are members of subgroups protected under federal employment discrimination law. Under its due process clause, a licensing test must be shown to be "rationally related" to the purposes it is designed to serve, namely the assessment of occupational competence for the protection of the public welfare; the licensing test and its use must not be "arbitrary and capricious."

It is possible that a set of federal test validation requirements may be relevant in a Fourteenth Amendment challenge to occupational licensing activities, even though the statute under which such requirements were issued has generally been held not to be applicable to such activities. Specifically, even though Title VII of the Civil Rights Act of 1964, an employment discrimination statute, has generally been held to be inapplicable in lawsuits against occupational licensing agencies, the "Uniform Guidelines on Employee Selection Procedures" (Equal Employment Opportunity Commission and others, 1978) bear on the question of the job-relatedness of the test being used in a way which is relevant in licensing, as well as in employment directly. The guidelines, as applied in employment testing cases, come into play following a showing that the employment selection procedure challenged, such as a test, has been shown to disproportionately exclude members of racial, ethnic, or gender subgroups protected by Title VII. To the extent that the guidelines' validation requirements may be consistent with accepted measurement principles and may be appropriate in the occupational licensing context, they provide some guidance as to legally defensible test validation, though the influence in occupational licensing test litigation has yet to be established.

Ensuring the Integrity of the Testing Process

Test Security. Because of the important role that licensing tests play in the ability of individuals to practice their chosen professions or occupations and earn a living, the integrity of the testing process is of critical importance. In turn, the pressures brought by some individuals and companies challenge even the most dedicated testing firms and licensing agencies to ensure equitable treatment and fair results to all participants.

For a licensing testing program to function properly, it must be able to establish, with reasonable degrees of certainty, that all candidates who are taking the examination have the same testing experience and that some are not advantaged by prior knowledge of the test or opportunities to cheat or to influence the score results. This requires what is referred to as "secure testing," in which the content of test forms is not known prior to testing, significant steps are taken to ensure fair treatment for all, and strong efforts are made to prevent and detect cheating.

Testing security is critical at three major points in the testing cycle: before testing, during testing, and after testing.

Before administration, test security is concerned primarily with keeping anyone from getting advance information regarding individual questions or the test itself. This is typically accomplished by adherence to standards and monitoring of access to tests and questions during development, limiting access at carefully screened printers, and controlling shipment and storage of tests.

During testing, there must be provisions for physical separation of candidates to reduce opportunities for copying, careful and trained supervision and proctoring, and careful and accurate checking of candidate identification prior to distribution of testing materials. Procedures for reporting irregularities and suspected cheating must exist and be adhered to.

Finally, after test administration, procedures should exist for following up on supervisors' reports of irregularities and suspected cheating before or during test administration. When cheating is suspected, appropriate internal and external checks must be made to establish whether or not the integrity of the scores is in question. In such circumstances the issue of fairness to test-takers and the public comes into play. At the same time, it is important that procedures followed in such cases are as fair as possible to the individuals involved and yet reduce the likelihood that unqualified practitioners are licensed as a result of cheating.

While usually seen as reasonable by the test-maker and the licensing agency, test security often conflicts with the views of some test-takers. So-called "truth in testing" laws in effect in two states, New York (Education Law, Article 7a, Section 342) and California (Education Code, Part 65, Chapter 3), which to date have affected only educational admissions tests, are a reaction, in part, to attempts by testing firms to control access to test forms even after administration. They typically require post-administration disclosure of the test forms used. While this does not directly weaken test security and may indeed have a positive impact on test quality, it affects the cost of developing tests, particularly those tests which tap knowledge of subject matter areas, such as would be involved in licensing testing, whose question base may well be relatively limited compared with the question bases of aptitude testing programs for educational admissions. Unless the money is spent to develop and use new forms instead of reusing released forms, the result will be the compromise of the test program security. Some states allow candidates to review the test they took under close supervision and secure conditions. While it is possible that such procedures weaken test security, their effect is generally considered minor.

For some small-volume licensing programs with low budgets and frequent administrations, security can quickly become nonexistent when the same form is repeatedly administered to candidates. In these circumstances, licensing agencies need to consider the trade-offs between the integrity of the measurement instrument (test security), and cost, method of testing, frequency of testing, volume, and other factors. In these cases it may not be possible to satisfy all the desired goals, and some compromises will need to be made.

Quality Control. Another critical aspect in ensuring the quality of the testing process is the quality control procedures used in the test development process, during the test administration, in scoring and reporting, and in dealing with faulty items and other errors.

The test development process must include sufficient review and editing to ensure, to the extent possible, that each item has one and only one correct response and that no ambiguity or other confusion has entered into the wording of the question. Test production must include procedures to avoid errors in printing or book assembly.

Standardized test administration procedures must be spelled out in writing and controls put in place to ensure that they are being followed. Announced and unannounced observations of test centers and supervisors are often employed. Matters such as timing limits, instructions, monitoring, proper identification procedures, and collection of testing materials should all be standardized and reviewed periodically.

The actual scoring and reporting of test results requires careful control of the statistical and computer procedures, to ensure appropriateness, accuracy, consistency, and adequate monitoring of results. Item statistics should be checked, and subject-matter specialists should review any items with questionable statistics. Procedures should be in place to monitor and control the quality of the statistical and score output before licenses are issued.

In spite of everything that can be devised and implemented, isolated errors can still occur, and some of these will affect the scores of individuals taking licensing tests. The integrity of the testing agency and the licensing agency in the handling of these errors, when they are identified, is what protects the integrity of the testing process. In spite of the cost, embarrassment, and potential for legal action resulting from an error not caught before scores were reported, expeditious, fair, and sensitive action on the part of the testing agency and the licensing agency to correct errors is necessary if the total process is to maintain its integrity.

Ensuring Sound Interpretation and Use of Test Results

Setting Standards. Unlike most employment selection or educational admissions decisions, licensing decisions generally do not involve comparisons of individuals' results. Rather, they are basically concerned with whether or not a particular applicant for a license has met the standard established for the test. How high an individual's passing score was or how close an individual came to failing or passing is of no basic concern.

In this circumstance, the point at which the pass-fail "cut score," or standard, is set becomes critical to the interpretation of the test results. Regardless of who develops, administers, or scores the test, the licensing agency is ultimately responsible for setting the standard and for its appropriateness. It reflects, along with the test content, the "minimum competency" standard the agency is charged with upholding for the profession or occupation being licensed.

In setting the standard for the test, it is critical to the fairness and legal defensibility of the licensing process that there be a documented rationale for whatever standard is set. The use of the traditional academic standard of 70 percent correct to pass the test, if it has no other rationale to support it, is not professionally defensible and is vulnerable to legal challenge. Similarly, a standard that shifts with the judgment of the licensing body following availability of the test results is likely to lead to charges of manipulating the system to control the flow of licensed persons into the profession or occupation, for economic rather than public interest reasons.

All methods for setting cut scores involve judgment. There are no totally empirical approaches, because even those which use data require judgments about how that distribution will be used in setting the pass point. The two most common approaches are: (1) judgments about where in the distribution of scores of the population the pass point will be set and (2) judgments about anticipated performance on individual items which, when combined, lead to a total score judged to represent minimally competent performance.

Establishing in advance a cut-score point of, for example, 1.5 standard deviations below the mean for the group taking the test reduces the viability of a charge to manipulate the system to control the flow into the profession. However, it establishes a finite limit on the number of individuals who can pass the test at any single administration because a certain percentage of the candidates will fail regardless of their scores, since by statistical definition there will usually be individuals with scores below 1.5 standard deviations. In addition, if the pass point is totally dependent on the population taking the test at a particular administration, the actual quality of the failing and passing populations can vary significantly from test administration to test administration. Thus, a score of 75 might easily pass a candidate in an administration in which the distribution of scores placed that score above 1.5 standard deviations from the mean but in another administration could fail the candidate if the distribution placed that score below the pass point. In addition, this relative approach can work only if there is a sufficient number of test-takers to produce a reliable distribution of scores, though the standard from one or more previous administrations could be used.

The normative approach involves making a judgment about the percentage of persons in a relatively large reference group who would meet the expected standard and set the cut score at that point on the test. This is most easily accomplished when some measure, such as course grades, is available for the members of the reference group to quantify the judgmental process. The judgment should be based on some other information than the test results.

Another method for determining a cut score sets the standard in terms of the test and not of the population taking the test. It focuses on judgments about individual questions or on the correct answer and alternative responses, which, taken together, define the score that the minimally acceptable applicant should earn on the test. This can be modified in terms of the standard error of measurement associated with such judgments and other factors. It results, in contrast to the relative or normative approach, in a score which for any particular administration could have everyone passing or everyone failing, if everyone fell above or below the cut score.

There are several basic methods for setting cut scores that are based on judgments at the item level. The reader is referred to a comprehensive review of these methods contained in *Passing Scores: A Manual for Setting Standards of Performance on Educational and Occupational Tests* by Livingston and Zieky (1982). These approaches permit setting the cut score prior to administration of the test. They have generally proven to be highly defensible, because they provide a clear rationale for the score selected.

Test Bias. One of the most widely discussed and least understood issues in testing revolves around the term "test bias." It is generally used in the context of the test allegedly being "biased" against a protected group. Too often this is interpreted to mean that if the protected group (females, minorities, the handicapped) score lower as a group than nonminorities, the test is biased. Another interpretation of test bias is that the language or content of the test is biased against women or minorities in the use of terms, choice of examples, and so on, in which the special groups because of their status have not had the same opportunity to be exposed to the materials.

Problems that fit into the latter interpretation are relatively easy to identify and to correct or prevent. It involves a careful review of the test by individuals who are sensitive to and trained in the recognition of racial and sexist language and content problems. At least one testing company, ETS, routinely requires all of its tests to be reviewed according to published guidelines designed to assist reviewers in identifying questions which are potentially offensive or inappropriate for subgroup members; subgroup members participate in these special "test sensitivity" reviews. Modifications are made where necessary before the tests are published or used.

Differences in performance between, for example, minorities and nonminorities on a test are easy to identify, but they do not necessarily mean that the test is biased. To the extent that the test results produce a valid and reliable picture of performance that is also reflected in the criterion performance, there is little basis for alleging that a test is unfair or biased.

In employment selection situations the "4/5 rule" is used to define adverse impact in the legal context. That is, if the hiring rate of applicants from a protected group is less than four fifths the rate for applicants from the minority group, adverse impact is said to exist, and the burden of proof that the test or other selection instrument is not discriminating unfairly shifts from the plaintiff to the defendant. At this point, the validity of the examination becomes critical. If it can be shown that the differences in performance between a protected group and a nonprotected group are a function of a valid test and testing situation, illegal discrimination does not exist. For example, if a test that shows adverse impact can be shown to have high content or criterion-related validity, the adverse impact can be shown to be a function of the job and the differential preparation or self-selection of individuals for it, and not due to bias in the test itself.

A more complete discussion of the legal aspects of licensing, including those related to testing, is covered in Chapter Five. It is sufficient to note here that if care is taken in the development of the tests to avoid bias in language and content, if the test has proven validity, and if the test results are properly used, the test producer and the licensing agency can feel relatively confident that the test will withstand legal challenge even if protected groups score lower on it than do nonprotected groups.

Equating Test Forms. When several forms of a test are used in making licensing decisions, as they normally must be in order to protect the security of the examination, the fact that a score on one form of the test may not mean the same as a similar score on a second form of the test must be faced. In spite of the best efforts of test producers, it is almost impossible to create two or more forms of a test that are exactly equal in terms of difficulty level. This being the case, unless special efforts are made, a score of 50 out of 60 items correct on one form will not have the same meaning as a score of 50 out of 60 on another form. If 50 correct is the standard for licensure, the individual scoring 50 correct on the easier form would need to know less than the individual scoring 50 on the harder form of the test. More important, it is likely that a person who scored slightly below 50 on the more difficult test and failed would have scored 50 or higher on the easier form of the test and passed. Therefore, unless special steps are taken to correct for these differences, licensing agencies are treating applicants for licensure unfairly and may be open to serious legal challenge.

The measurement approach to dealing with this problem is called *equating,* a statistical practice followed by many, although not all, professional testing organizations. While a number of techniques are used to accomplish the result, all equating procedures are intended to adjust the score results of forms of the test so that a score on one form means essentially (within the error range associated with the technique used) what the same score on another form of the test means. Equating is usually accompanied by *scaling,* or the creation of a particular score scale, such as 10 to 50 or 1 to 9, to which the raw scores, the number of questions answered correctly, are converted. In combination with equating, scaling provides a standard and clear method for providing information about individuals' performance on multiple forms of a test.

For the most part, the licensing agency need not be concerned about the type of equating method used. However, one cautionary note should be given. One of the newer generic equating techniques is called *item response theory* or *IRT* equating. This family of equating techniques is based on obtaining question or item parameters on each item and then establishing the equating parameters often prior to the actual operational administration of the test. While the approach is sound and has many advantages, it makes one fundamental assumption which should be tested before use. That is the assumption that the test being equated is *unidimensional*—that it has only one dimension or that its content, when examined statistically, can be shown to be measuring only one thing. If, for example, a licensing test is measuring several distinct things and not just one, the equating based on an IRT approach will not be valid. In some cases, test producers will commit to using an IRT equating approach without testing the unidimensionality of the test being equated. Licensing agencies should ascertain whether or not this assumption has been tested before accepting an IRT equating approach as a viable one.

In some cases, it is not possible to equate because of the small number of applicants taking the test at any one time. When this is the case, equating can be omitted due to impracticality, and the parallel construction of test forms can be relied on to reduce the error as much as possible. Where equating is feasible, however, it should be used, since it greatly enhances the fairness and legal defensibility of the test.

Feedback. The kind of feedback on test performance given to the individuals taking a test should be related directly to the purpose and intended use of the test. Testing agencies should take into account the possible misuse of the feedback information and carefully weigh what information is needed rather than what can be provided.

Because of the possibility that some individuals and firms may attempt to use licensing test information to make employment selection decisions, some test producers and licensing test sponsors do not report the actual scores of passing candidates to the candidates or anyone other than the licensing agency. (See Burns, 1983, for fuller discussion of differences and responsibilities.) Because the test is intended to measure minimum competency and has not been validated for use in employment selection (there is no evidence that those who score higher on the licensing test will be more successful in a particular occupation or profession), using the test results for employment selection would be a misuse of the test and could lead to legal problems.

At the same time, an applicant who has not passed the examination needs to know his or her score on the test and, to the extent possible, the areas of weakness in the test content. For this reason, many licensing testing programs report only a passing notice, without an actual test score, to the passing candidate but report actual scores and performance data on subsets of the test content to failing candidates. This permits failing candidates to concentrate their study in the areas where they need it most. It should be recognized, however, that because there are usually only relatively few items in each content area of the test, meaningful subscores often cannot be reported. Rather, only basic information, such as the number missed out of the number asked in any area or some idea of relative performance on a content area, can be provided.

Questions a Licensing Administrator Might Ask

Most licensing agency directors and staff are not measurement experts. Some, in larger states and departments, may have measurement personnel on staff or make use of outside consultants, and most make some use of national licensing testing programs. In these settings, it is not important that the licensing administrators have testing expertise. What is important is that they be aware of the issues and potential problems surrounding testing for occupational licensure and know what questions to ask. The following list provides some questions that a licensing administrator might wish to raise with his or her own staff or with the providers and sponsors of national licensing testing programs.

- Is the basic purpose of the test stated with sufficient clarity and precision so that there is no room for misunderstanding what the test is supposed to accomplish?
- What provisions have been made to ensure job-relatedness?
- Are the test specifications related to the definition of job relevance? Is this documented? Are the item linkages to the specifications and the job analysis documented?
- How was the method of testing determined? Does it meet the objectives of the agency in terms of cost, timeliness, psychometric soundness, appropriateness, and so on?
- How can I be confident that all aspects of the testing procedure are psychometrically sound? Are there built-in provisions for periodically reviewing the test content, reliability, and

other aspects of the program and making adjustments as necessary?

• Have all the elements of test security been attended to?

• Are there adequate provisions for quality control? Are there responsible and acceptable provisions for handling errors?

• Has a defensible rationale been developed for the passing standard established? Is it documented?

• What provisions have been made to attempt to eliminate bias in the test? Are they adequate?

• Does some method of equating the test scores between forms exist? Is it adequate?

• Which professional standards does the test or licensing program purport to meet? How is attainment of these standards demonstrated?

• What type of feedback will be provided to the test-taker? Is the feedback appropriate and adequate?

• Does the overall licensing testing program meet the needs of the licensing agency? Will it meet legal and professional standards?

The basic purpose of this book and of this chapter in particular is to increase the licensing administrator's awareness and understanding of the issues and potential problems surrounding testing for occupational licensing. Careful attention to the responses received in answer to the suggested questions should enhance the quality of licensing programs.

References

American Psychological Association. *Standards for Educational and Psychological Tests.* Washington, D.C.: American Psychological Association, 1974.

Burns, R. L. "Roles, Responsibilities, and Relationships of National Testing Organizations and Licensing Groups." *National Clearinghouse on Examination Information,* 1983, *1* (4), 10-20.

Educational Testing Service. *ETS Standards for Quality and Fairness.* Princeton, N.J.: Educational Testing Service, 1983.

Equal Employment Opportunity Commission and others. "Adoption by Four Agencies of Uniform Guidelines on Employment Selection Procedures." *Federal Register,* 1978, *43,* 38290-38315.

Livingston, S. A., and Zieky, M. J. *Passing Scores: A Manual for Setting Standards of Performance on Educational and Occupational Tests.* Princeton, N.J.: Educational Testing Service, 1982.

National Commission for Health Certifying Agencies. *Criteria for Membership.* Washington, D.C.: U.S. Government Printing Office, 1977.

Subkoviak, M. J. "Decision-Consistency Approaches." In R. A. Berk (Ed.), *Criterion-Referenced Measurement: The State of the Art.* Baltimore, Md.: Johns Hopkins University Press, 1980.

Additional Readings

Anastasi, A. *Psychological Testing.* New York: Macmillan, 1982.

Angoff, W. H. "Scales, Norms, and Equivalent Scores." In R. L. Thorndike (Ed.), *Educational Measurement.* Washington, D.C.: American Council on Education, 1971.

Gael, S. *Job Analysis: A Guide to Assessing Work Activities.* San Francisco: Jossey-Bass, 1983.

Holland, P. W., and Rubin, D. W. *Test Equating.* New York: Academic Press, 1982.

Kane, M. T. "The Validity of Licensure Examinations." *American Psychologist,* 1982, *37* (8), 911-918.

Knapp, J., and Sharon, A. *A Compendium of Assessment Techniques.* Princeton, N.J.: Educational Testing Service, 1975.

Lloyd, J. S. (Ed.). *Oral Examinations in Medical Specialty Board Certification.* Chicago: American Board of Medical Specialties, 1983.

McCormick, E. J. "Job and Task Analysis." In M. D. Dunnette (Ed.), *Handbook of Industrial and Organizational Psychology.* Chicago: Rand McNally, 1976.

Rosenfeld, M., and Thornton, R. F. *A Case Study in Job Analysis Methodology.* Princeton, N.J.: Educational Testing Service, 1976.

3

Definitions and Strategies for Validating Licensure Examinations

Michael T. Kane

Validity consists of the evidence supporting the proposed interpretation of examination scores. Because a candidate's score on a licensure examination is typically interpreted as indicating the candidate's readiness to practice safely and effectively, the evidence for validity should establish a relationship between scores on the examination and readiness for practice. The issue, then, is the nature of this relationship and the evidence needed to establish that the intended relationship exists.

The evidence included in an argument for a particular interpretation of examination scores may take many forms. The validity of licensure examinations is typically discussed under three headings: content validity, criterion validity, and construct validity. Evidence for content validity supports the interpretation of scores in terms of a degree of competence in some content domain.

Evidence for criterion validity supports the interpretation of scores as predictors of some criterion of interest. In the case of licensure examinations, the criterion may be a measure of future performance (for example, ratings of performance in practice), or it may be a score on some current criterion measure (for example, a performance examination simulating some aspects of practice situations). These two subclasses of criterion validity are called predictive validity and criterion-related validity, respectively.

Construct validity supports the interpretation of test scores in terms of certain assumptions about what is being measured and indicates that the test scores reflect an attribute defined by the assumptions. The methods of construct validity are especially useful where the attribute being measured is implicitly defined by a theory that incorporates the assumptions used to generate validity evidence (see Cronbach and Meehl, 1955). However, construct validity can also be viewed as subsuming content validity and criterion validity. In criterion validity, the assumption being investigated is that readiness for practice as measured by the examination is related, usually linearly, to subsequent performance in practice. In content validity, the assumption being tested is that the test measures knowledge of a domain that is important for performance in practice.

Because validity is associated with the interpretation of measurements (Cronbach, 1971), evidence that supports the intended interpretation of test scores is important in establishing validity. There are two common interpretations of the scores on licensure examinations. First, they can be interpreted as providing predictions of an examinee's future professional performance. Second, they can be interpreted as providing evidence of an examinee's present competence on specific abilities that are needed for practice. I have argued (Kane, in press) that the second of these two interpretations is the more appropriate interpretation for licensure examinations. Manning (1978) has made a similar argument in discussing the legal aspects of validation for employment testing.

Scores as Predictors of Future Performance

The interpretation of licensure examination scores as predictors of future performance in practice is appealing because it implies a high degree of utility for the licensure process. To the extent that this interpretation is applied to a licensure examination, arguments for validity would emphasize predictive validity (Hogan, 1979; Hecht, 1979). However, there are a number of serious impediments to the effective use of criterion validity in validating licensure examinations and, therefore, to the viability of the predictive interpretation.

The Criterion Problem. The usefulness of predictive validity for licensure examinations is limited greatly by the fact that criteria of proven validity are not available for licensure examinations. The development and validation of a criterion measure of professional performance presents fundamental conceptual problems as well as great practical difficulties. In part because practice requires a high level of professional judgment for effective performance, the distinction between good practice and poor practice is not clear-cut in most cases (for example, see Strupp, Hadley, and Gomes-Schwartz, 1977), and the development of general measures of the quality of practice that are comprehensive, reliable, and valid is probably not possible for most professions. Assumptions about the validity of the criterion are likely to be questionable at best, and to the extent that the validity of the criterion is questionable, any conclusions drawn from a predictive validity study would be questionable.

The seriousness of the criterion problem is illustrated by the experience of the National Board of Medical Examiners, as reported by Hubbard (1971). After three years of attempting to develop a reliable bedside valuation using real clients, they found that when one observer rated a candidate in one situation and another observer rated the same candidate in a different situation, interrater agreement was at the chance level. In another study, Hoffman (1977) found that an oral examination based on a physician's interaction with a client had low reliability because of variability in the results from one situation to another. Where such results occur, one must conclude that the ratings are, to a large extent, measuring characteristics of the raters, the situations, or other contextual factors rather than the competence of the candidate.

Technical Problems. In addition to the criterion problem, there are two technical issues that limit the application of criterion validity to licensure examinations. First, licensure is not intended to indicate readiness for a specific task or job, but rather for a wide range of activities in a variety of settings. A criterion validity study showing that a test predicts performance in one setting does not necessarily demonstrate that the test also predicts performance in other settings, and it is not clear whether evidence for criterion validity can be generalized from one setting to another (Cronbach, 1980a; Hunter, 1980). For a licensure examination, therefore, the logic of criterion validity could require not one validity study but a large number of validity studies—one for each of the settings in which licensed practitioners might work.

A second technical problem is that the data needed to evaluate the predictive validity of a licensure examination are not generally available, because those who do not pass the examination are not allowed to practice. The crucial question for a study of the predictive validity of a licensure examination is whether those who pass the examination are more likely to be safe and effective in practice than those who fail, and this question is not answered by a correlation coefficient based only on passing candidates. A more appropriate index of the predictive validity of a licensing examination would be a measure of the agreement between the pass/fail dichotomy on the licensure examination and a competent/incompetent dichotomy in subsequent practice; however, an index, such as coefficient kappa (Cohen, 1960), that would address this issue cannot be estimated without having criterion scores for those who fail the examination as well as for those who pass. Attempts to collect such data might be considered unethical (and probably illegal) in many professions.

Scores as Measures of Critical Abilities

Alternatively, licensure examination scores can be interpreted in terms of a domain of knowledge and skills; that is, in terms of critical abilities that are necessary, although not sufficient, for effective performance in practice. Abilities are considered *critical* to the extent that their absence would be a serious limitation in the practice of the profession. The critical abilities for a profession typically include cognitive abilities involving knowledge and the ability to apply knowledge, as well as psychomotor skills involving the ability to apply various skills for clients.

In interpreting licensure examinations in terms of critical abilities, the connection between test scores and performance in practice involves two steps. The test scores are interpreted as indicating overall level of proficiency in a domain of critical abilities, and proficiency in the domain is viewed as necessary for effective performance in practice.

Critical Abilities and the Department of Learning. What kind of abilities should be considered critical for a profession? The *American College Dictionary* defines a profession as a "vocation requiring knowledge of some department of learning or science." Presumably many of the critical abilities will be drawn from the department of learning or science associated with the profession. The abilities may be quite general (for example, communication skills) or quite specific (such as the ability to carry out a particular procedure). Including a particular ability in a licensure examination would be justified by evidence connecting the ability to client outcomes, and typically this evidence would be drawn from the department of learning for the profession. The inclusion of some abilities is based on empirical evidence (for example, ability to carry out medical procedures that are based on clinical trials). In other cases, abilities are justified by logical analysis and by procedural rules (for example, in law). Specification of test content in terms of critical abilities does not require an exhaustive listing of the abilities required for practice, but each ability should be clearly related to practice.

Combining Validation Strategies. The validation of licensure examinations as measures of critical abilities involves aspects of content validity, criterion validity, and construct validity. The evidence supporting the interpretation of test scores in terms of a domain of critical abilities would include many elements of content validity.

The evidence relating critical abilities to client outcomes

can be interpreted as providing indirect criterion validation of the licensure examination. Where a predictive validity study seeks to determine the relationship between performance on a test and some criterion of future performance for each individual, the critical abilities approach depends on empirical relationships between various abilities and client outcomes averaged over large numbers of professionals and clients (in clinical trials) or on rational analysis. That is, the critical abilities approach depends heavily on the theoretical and empirical content of the department of learning associated with the profession.

In its emphasis on the testing of assumptions embedded in the department of learning, the critical abilities approach requires several types of arguments/analyses. This combination of different types of evidence can be viewed as an example of construct validity, where the construct at issue, professional competence, is defined in terms of the network of theoretical and empirical relationships incorporated in the department of learning.

A basic assumption of this discussion is that the validation of licensure examinations should be tailored to the purpose of these examinations and should be consistent with the intended interpretations of the examinations. Since none of the three standard validation strategies (content, criterion, and construct) provides a perfect fit to the interpretation of licensure examinations as measures of critical abilities, these terms will not generally be used in the remainder of this paper. Instead, the evidence needed to support the validity of a licensure examination will be discussed in relation to the interpretation given to the examinations.

Structure of Validity Argument for Critical Abilities Interpretation

The structure of validity arguments involving the critical ability approach is quite simple, including two premises and a conclusion:

- Premise 1: Because the critical abilities are necessary for effective performance, individuals who lack the critical abilities to a substantial degree will not be able to perform adequately in practice.

- Premise 2: Individuals who have low scores on the examination lack the critical abilities to a substantial degree.
- Conclusion: Individuals who have low scores on the examination will not be able to perform adequately in practice.

Although the structure of the argument is simple, the development of the argument in a specific case is not simple because it requires substantial evidence for the two premises. The second premise involves issues usually considered under the label of "content validity" (that is, relationship between test and domain) and issues of standard setting (that is, the meaning of saying that individuals lack the critical abilities "to a substantial degree").

The first premise assumes a relationship between the critical abilities and performance in practice. If it were necessary to start from scratch, establishing the relationship between critical abilities and performance in practice could be an enormous undertaking; a large-scale study is often required to establish the relationship between a particular intervention (for example, polio vaccination) and client outcomes (incidence of polio).

Fortunately, it is not necessary to start from scratch. The department of learning for a profession generally specifies relationships between professional interventions and outcomes. In fact, much of the research effort included in the relevant department of learning can be interpreted as an attempt to identify critical elements in the practice of the profession.

Premise 1: The Relationship of Critical Abilities to Practice

Looking first at the components inherent in the first premise, the abilities included in the domain of critical abilities measured by the examination should be "critical" in the sense that they have a significant influence on client outcomes, and any ability required for licensure should be explicitly linked to client outcomes. The linkage may be based on clinical research, on logical analysis, or on a combination of the two, but it should be explicit.

Since some critical abilities will be more critical than others, the weight given to various content areas in defining the domain of critical abilities should reflect the importance of the content areas for practice. The importance of an ability depends on how often it is needed in practice (its frequency) and on how much difference it is likely to make in terms of client outcomes (its impact).

Frequency. The frequency of occurrence of a situation in professional practice is obviously one factor in determining how important it is that a practitioner be able to deal with the situation. For example, it is clearly appropriate that examinations for medical licensure in the United States devote considerable attention to heart disease, diabetes, cancer, and flu because they have a high rate of incidence.

Extensive data are available, for some professions at least, on the incidence and severity of various kinds of problems that professionals are likely to encounter in practice, such as data on the incidences of various medical conditions. Such data provide a good first approximation in describing the demands of practice.

Job analyses, which usually place heavy emphasis on frequency data (Williamson, 1979), enable us to refine our understanding of what professionals are called upon to do in practice. Data on how practitioners spend their working time are clearly relevant to the definitionof content domains for licensure examinations because they indicate the frequency with which various situations occur in practice. A limitation with data on how professionals spend their time is that the activities included in such data will vary in their importance relative to the purpose of licensure, protection of the public. For example, Williamson reports that 32 percent of a physician's time at work is spent on activities other than patient care. Therefore, job analyses generally collect data on practitioners' ratings of the importance as well as the frequency of various activities (see Gael, 1983; McCormick, 1979; Flanagan, 1954).

Although professional practitioners and content specialists necessarily have much to say about requirements for licensure, including examination content, the public and the public's representatives in state legislatures also have a major interest in such requirements. Job analyses indicate what is going on in practice, but they do not necessarily indicate what should be going on. Given that various activities are given different levels of emphasis in practice, the appropriateness of this distribution of emphasis is still open to question, and the resolution of such issues involves complex judgments.

Impact. The second component in evaluating the relative importance of different abilities is the gravity of the possible consequences of the situations that require the ability. Rakel has stressed the importance of the "harmful if missed" category in medical practice. "There is a justifiable need to test more heavily on problems that have a high morbidity and fall into the 'uncommon but harmful if missed' category. Because of their serious nature, they deserve greater representation in an examination than practice surveys indicate" (Rakel, 1979, p. 93). Given that the purpose of licensure is to protect the public, the "harmful if missed" category would seem to be especially important for licensure examinations.

Working from data on the frequency of specific situations, decisions about the knowledge and skills needed to deal effectively with these situations and the likely impact of various interventions on client outcomes should be based to a large extent on the relevant department of learning. The department of learning provides information on the causes, likely courses of development, and appropriate interventions for the situations encountered in professional practice. Such information provides a basis for identifying knowledge and skill required to deal effectively with the situations that arise in practice (as documented by job analysis).

For many professions the linkage between critical abilities and client outcomes has a large empirical component. The requirement that pharmacists be able to dispense drugs correctly is based on clinical research relating dosage to the effectiveness and safety of the drugs. In some professions, the linkage between various abilities and client outcomes is based mainly on logical analysis. A strong logical case can be made for the linkage between knowledge of the law and effectiveness as a lawyer.

Where evidence linking an ability to client outcomes is less straightforward than it is for these simple examples, decisions about criticality become more complicated, and professional judgment is needed to select a particular approach for each client. If there are several approaches to some issue of professional practice and the evidence does not consistently favor one approach, it would still be reasonable to require that candidates for licensure know enough about the various approaches to recognize their potential benefits and limitations. Given the purpose of licensure, it is especially important that practitioners be aware of any dangers inherent in various interventions.

For many areas of practice, mastery of a domain of knowledge that is relevant to a broad range of situations may be required to inform the practitioners' decisions about how to handle specific situations. That is, an approach to validity based on critical abilities should not be viewed as an attempt to reduce highly developed, complex content domains to a set of discrete pieces of knowledge linked to specific practice situations.

In general, empirical job analyses are particularly useful in providing information about the kinds of situations that will be encountered in practice, while the department of learning for the profession is a more reliable source of information about how these situations should be handled. In weighting various critical abilities, both empirical job analysis and the department of learning have major roles to play.

Premise 2: The Relationship of Examination Scores to Critical Abilities

The second premise states that individuals with low scores on the examination lack the critical abilities to a substantial degree. In order to provide adequate support for this premise, a number of issues must be addressed.

Coverage of the Domain of Critical Abilities. Since licensure laws typically qualify the professional to deal with a broad range of problems in a variety of settings, the results of the licensure examination are likely to be interpreted as indicating candidates' command of a correspondingly broad range of abilities. Although it is usually not possible to test the relevant domain exhaustively, the examination content should provide reasonable coverage of the domain as a whole and reflect the importance of different parts of the domain. The test specifications typically used to develop licensure examinations are designed to ensure a representative sampling of content.

The content of the licensing examination must also be consistent with the scope of practice specified in the legislation authorizing licensure for the profession. Although the laws governing the scope of professional practice may be stated in general terms that leave considerable latitude for interpretation, the legal definition of professional practice still limits the content for a licensure examination to some extent. It would be inappropriate for a licensure examination to require demonstration of a skill that is legally prohibited in practice.

Minimizing Effect of Extraneous Factors. The interpretation of test scores as measures of critical abilities assumes that differences in scores are due to differences among candidates in their attainment of the critical abilities. Cronbach (1980b) points out the need "to establish that an achievement test contains no irrelevant difficulty, if we are to say that it measures command of certain subject matter" (p. 106). To ensure that tests of the critical abilities are measuring what they claim to measure, plausible alternative hypotheses should be investigated.

Some potential competing hypotheses are examined under the heading of reliability or generalizability (Brennan, 1983; Cronbach and others, 1972; Kane, 1982b). Measures of stability address the competing hypothesis that observed scores are a function of the occasion on which the measurement is made. Measures of interrater reliability address the hypothesis that scores are largely determined by the observer rather than by the candidate's performance. Measures of internal homogeneity (for example, KR-20, coefficient alpha) or parallel-forms reliability address the competing hypothesis that the choice of a particular set of test items strongly influences the outcome.

Standard test development procedures (for example, see

Ebel, 1972) are designed to minimize the chances that candidates who have the ability being tested by an item will get the item wrong or that candidates who do not have the ability being tested will get the item right. Poorly constructed tests are likely to give an unfair advantage to candidates who are skillful at taking tests.

A potentially serious problem for some types of measurement procedures is the presence of a response set favoring socially desirable responses. Affective traits, which are defined in terms of typical performance rather than the best possible performance, are especially subject to response sets. A pattern of "correct" answers to questions about ethical issues may reflect a conscious effort to give the "right" answers rather than a commitment to ethical behavior. To the extent possible, testing procedures should be designed to minimize the influence of response sets.

It is also important to ensure that the language used in the test does not constitute an artificial barrier to performance. Except for the use of technical vocabulary, the reading level of the examination should be kept sufficiently low so that anyone with the abilities required for practice will be able to read it. Similarly, the instructions for the examination should be as clear and simple as possible (especially when the instructions are unusual, as they often are for simulations).

It is important to avoid any extraneous factors that could cause minority or women candidates who had developed the critical abilities being tested to get items wrong. Although important content should not be omitted simply to eliminate differences between subgroups, the wording of items should be reviewed to avoid any source of bias that would unnecessarily interfere with the performance of subgroups within the population (Schmeiser, 1982).

Appropriateness of Cognitive Level of Items. Although the definition quoted earlier refers to "knowledge of some department of learning or science," it is clear that to be safe and effective in practice, the professional must also be able to use this knowledge to solve problems. The professional must be able to apply elements from the department of learning or science to the situations that arise in practice.

If the questions in a licensure examination require the application of knowledge to specific situations, the performance required of the candidate taking the examination is closer to that required in practice than would be the case if the examination involved simple recall of facts. To the extent that the performance required on the licensure examination is similar to the performance required in practice, inferences drawn from test performance to readiness for practice are more direct and therefore easier to justify.

Appropriateness of Level of Proficiency Required. For a licensure examination that measures a selected set of critical abilities rather than all of the characteristics required for good practice, it is important that the standards on the examination not be set unreasonably high. Although some level of competence in an ability (research skills, for example) may be necessary for practice, it is not always true that higher levels of the ability will lead to improved performance.

In general, licensure examinations emphasize knowledge and the ability to apply knowledge because these abilities can be measured accurately with written tests. Since cognitive abilities are important for professional practice, this is reasonable, but if the standards for cognitive abilities are artificially high, the licensing examination may exclude many candidates who would make good practitioners.

Serving the Public Function. As noted earlier, to validate an interpretation for an examination is to provide evidence that the interpretation is justified. Since licensure examinations serve a public function, the evidence for validity should be available for review by the public that licensure procedures are designed to protect.

In addition, the release of sample copies of the examination, where this is feasible, would serve a useful function in informing discussion and debate about licensure. The periodic release of retired forms of the examinations would provide an opportunity for external review of examination content, format, and quality. Complete disclosure of all examinations is not justified in most cases because of the costs involved and because the additional benefits of complete disclosure compared to partial disclosure would be marginal.

Standard Setting

The generally recommended procedures for establishing passing scores for licensure examinations are based on the judgments of content experts (for example, see Angoff, 1971; Ebel, 1972; Nedelsky, 1954). A limitation of the judgment-based standard-setting procedures as they are usually defined is that they do not yield an interpretation of what the standards mean in terms of what passing candidates can do. In the Angoff procedure, for example, expert judges are asked to consider the expected level of performance on each item (the probability of answering the item correctly) of hypothetical "minimally competent candidates." The judges are instructed to assign a minimum passing level (MPL) to each item in terms of the probability that a minimally competent candidate could answer that item correctly. Since the cutoff score for the examination is simply the sum of the MPLs for the individual items, it will depend on the sample of items and on the sample of raters.

Unless a behavioral interpretation of the test scores is available, the results of the Angoff procedure do not indicate the kind of behavior that distinguishes passing candidates from failing candidates. Although individual raters undoubtedly use some performance criteria in setting the MPL for each item, such as their individual experiences with persons they considered to be minimally competent, the judgment-based standard-setting procedures do not provide a mechanism for making these performance criteria explicit. Therefore, the interpretation of the resulting passing score depends on the criteria for selecting judges, and the burden of interpretation falls on the new reference population, the population of raters.

Of course, if some copies of the examination are made public along with the corresponding passing score, a reviewer could infer a behavioral interpretation by evaluating the content and difficulty of the examination and comparing the perceived difficulty to the passing score. The reviewer might even use one of the judgmental standard-setting procedures to obtain an independent estimate of the difficulty of the examination.

This concern about the interpretability of test scores in terms of explicit behavioral criteria is not new. Ebel (1962) suggested two methods for obtaining what he called "content standard test scores" over twenty years ago. One of his two methods is similar to the approach suggested in the following section. Nitko (1980) has described a number of ways in which test scores can be referenced to specific content, some of which could be applied to licensure examinations.

Improving the Interpretability of Standards. One way to make interpretive information more readily available would be to provide data about the differences in performance of passing candidates and failing candidates on a representative sample of items. For example, for a written examination interpretive data of this kind might indicate the proportion of passing candidates and the proportion of failing candidates who correctly answered a particular item.

A somewhat more sophisticated approach would be to provide graphs of the proportion of candidates answering an item correctly as a function of total score on the examination. Such graphs would provide detailed information about the implications of total test score for performance on that particular item and would therefore say something about the consequences of setting the passing score at a particular level. Graphs of this kind for a representative sample of items would provide a basis for the interpretation of the test scores in terms of candidate performance on the skills tested by the items.

A Check on Validity. In addition to its impact on interpretability, such approaches could lead to improvements in the setting of standards by providing a check on the internal consistency of the ratings. By examining the proportion of candidates who answer a given item correctly, we obtain an estimate of the probability that a minimally competent candidate, as defined by the Angoff procedure, can answer the item correctly. To the extent that this probability differs from the original MPL for the item, there is some inconsistency in the results.

Perfect consistency on judgments about MPLs for different items is not to be expected, and experience with the approach would be needed to determine what constitutes adequate agreement. However, major inconsistencies would suggest a possible problem; for example, if an item is important enough that the raters think that minimally competent candidates should be sure of answering it correctly (that is, the MPL is 1.0), but candidates with relatively low probabilities of answering the item correctly are passing the examination, the passing score may be too low. At the very least, such comparisons would inform the raters of the fallibility of the standard-setting procedure. The raters would also have the opportunity to re-examine the overall passing score in light of its implications for particular items.

This type of analysis would be a natural extension of the Angoff procedure, which is based on raters' judgments of the probability that a minimally competent candidate would get an item correct, but it could also be used for other commonly used judgmental standard-setting procedures. Because this approach has not yet been tried, I would not recommend it for immediate application, but I do think that it would be a fruitful topic for further research.

Summary of Issues of Validation

Matching the validation approach to the intended interpretation of the examinations requires an explicit description of the intended interpretation. I have argued that the interpretation of the examination scores in terms of abilities that are necessary for safe and effective practice is appropriate given the purpose of licensure, the protection of the public.

The argument for the validity of an interpretation in terms of critical abilities involves two components. The first component requires evidence that the abilities covered by the examination are critical for practice. Empirical job analyses are particularly useful in identifying situations that commonly arise in practice and in providing some data about the consequences of proper and improper handling of such situations. The department of learning for a profession provides information on how these situations should be handled to obtain optimal results. In combining these two sources of data, professional judgment plays a large role.

The second component requires evidence that the test scores reflect competence in the domain of critical abilities defined in the first step. Much of the evidence relevant to this issue is derived from the critical examination of the properties of the test in the light of plausible counter hypotheses about what the test measures.

Informing Public Discussion. Licensure is a public function, subject to public scrutiny. The appropriate scope of practice for licensed professionals is a matter of public policy that is encoded, at least in general terms, in licensure laws. Therefore, research on the validity of licensure examinations is more akin to policy research than it is to basic scientific research. The situations that practitioners should deal with, the types of interventions that they should employ, and the standard of skill to be expected in the implementation of these interventions are not questions that can be answered by empirical data; they are policy issues.

The public factor of licensure suggests that the results of validity studies that attempt simply to determine whether the test is valid will be less helpful ultimately than studies that provide information useful in making policy decisions and, more fundamentally, in informing debate about policy issues. Questions particularly relevant to policy decisions include:

- What types of situations occur most frequently in practice and/or have the most serious potential consequences?
- What abilities, including knowledge and skills, are needed to deal with these situations effectively?
- How well are these abilities taught and assessed in the educational programs preparing practitioners?
- How well does the examination assess competence in the critical abilities, and what sources of variance other than differences in competence (for example, reading level, response sets, ethnic bias) influence examination scores?
- What are the implications of setting standards at different levels?

Although research on the validity of licensure examinations will not resolve such issues, addressing questions like those just listed can promote informed debate.

References

Angoff, W. H. "Scales, Norms, and Equivalent Scores." In R. L. Thorndike (Ed.), *Educational Measurement.* Washington, D.C.: American Council on Education, 1971.

Brennan, R. L. *Elements of Generalizability Theory.* Iowa City, Iowa: American College Testing Program, 1983.

Cohen, J. "A Coefficient of Agreement for Nominal Scales." *Educational and Psychological Measurement,* 1960, *20,* 37-46.

Cronbach, L. J. "Test Validation." In R. L. Thorndike (Ed.), *Educational Measurement.* Washington, D.C.: American Council on Education, 1971.

Cronbach, L. J. "Selection Theory for a Political World." *Public Personnel Management,* 1980a, *9,* 37-50.

Cronbach, L. J. "Validity on Parole: How Can We Go Straight?" In W. B. Schrader (Ed.), *New Directions for Testing and Measurement: Measuring Achievement: Progress Over a Decade,* no. 5. San Francisco: Jossey-Bass, 1980b.

Cronbach, L. J., and Meehl, P. E. "Construct Validity in Psychological Tests." *Psychological Bulletin,* 1955, *52,* 281-302.

Cronbach, L. J., and others. *The Dependability of Behavioral Measurement.* New York: Wiley, 1972.

Ebel, R. L. "Content Standard Test Scores." *Educational and Psychological Measurement,* 1962, *22,* 15-25.

Ebel, R. L. *Essentials of Educational Measurement.* Englewood Cliffs, N.J.: Prentice-Hall, 1972.

Flanagan, J. C. "The Critical Incident Technique." *Psychological Bulletin,* 1954, *51,* 327-357.

Gael, S. *Job Analysis: A Guide to Assessing Work Activities.* San Francisco: Jossey-Bass, 1983.

Hecht, K. A. "Current Status and Methodological Problems of Validating Professional Licensing and Certification Exams." In M. A. Bunda and J. R. Sanders (Eds.), *Practices and Problems in Competency-Based Education.* Washington, D.C.: National Council on Measurement in Education, 1979.

Hoffman, P. "Continued Competence Assurance: Some Research and Measurement Considerations." In *Proceedings of a National Conference for Evaluating Competence in the Health Professions.* New York: Professional Examination Service, 1977.

Hogan, D. *The Regulation of Psychotherapists.* Vol. I: *A Study of the Philosophy and Practice of Professional Regulation.* Cambridge, Mass.: Ballinger, 1979.

Hubbard, J. P. *Measuring Medical Education: The Tests and Procedures of the National Board of Medical Examiners.* Philadelphia: Lea & Febiger, 1971.

Hunter, J. E. "Constuct Validity and Validity Generalization." In *Construct Validity in Psychological Measurement.* Princeton, N.J.: U.S. Office of Personnel Management and Educational Testing Service, 1980.

Kane, M. T. "The Validity of Licensure Examinations." *American Psychologist,* 1982a, *37,* 911-918.

Kane, M. T. "A Sampling Model for Validity." *Applied Psychological Measurement,* 1982b, *6,* 125-160.

Kane, M. T. "The Future of Testing for Licensure and Certification." In B. Plake and J. Witt (Eds.), *The Future of Testing and Measurement.* Hillsdale, N.J.: Erlbaum, in press.

McCormick, E. J. *Job Analysis: Methods and Applications.* New York: AMACOM, American Management Association, 1979.

Manning, W. H. "Test Validation and EEOC Requirements: Where We Stand." *Personnel,* 1978, pp. 70-77.

Nedelsky, L. "Absolute Grading Standards for Objective Tests." *Educational and Psychological Measurement, 14,* 1954, 3-19.

Nitko, A. J. "Distinguishing the Many Varieties of Criterion-Referenced Tests." *Review of Educational Research,* 1980, *50,* 461-485.

Rakel, R. E. "Defining Competence in Specialty Practice: The Need for Relevance." In *Definitions of Competence in Specialties of Medicine, Conference Proceedings.* Chicago: American Board of Medical Specialties, 1979.

Schmeiser, C. B. "Use of Experimental Design in Statistical Item Bias Studies." In R. A. Berk (Ed.), *Handbook of Meth-*

ods for Detecting Test Bias. Baltimore, Md.: Johns Hopkins University Press, 1982.

Strupp, H. H., Hadley, S. W., and Gomes-Schwartz, B. *Psychotherapy for Better or Worse, the Problem of Negative Effects.* New York: Aronson, 1977.

Williamson, J. W. "Improving Content Validity of Certification Procedures by Defining Competence in Specialty Practice: Directions, Resources, and Getting Started." In *Definitions of Competence in Specialties of Medicine, Conference Proceedings.* Chicago: American Board of Medical Specialties, 1979.

4

Determining Reliability and Validity of Licensure Examinations

James C. Impara
Howard W. Stoker

> To be useful, a psychological test must provide inferences about people, just as chemical and physical tests provide inferences about things. If litmus paper remains blue after being dipped into a solution, the solution is not an acid. If, however, a person who knows no chemistry . . . picks up a piece of ordinary blue paper to test a solution himself, any inferences he may draw will be worthless. In the same way, a properly constructed . . . test can provide valuable information when it is used in an appropriate situation; if a group of items are simply thrown together, however, the result may look like a test but probably will be useless.
>
> In order that a test be useful, then, it must differentiate between those who are desirable and those who are undesirable in a given situation. This requirement of a test is known as *validity*. . . . Although validity is the prime consideration, a good test must also be *reliable*. It measures a person's abilities in a constant way. A test with no reliability cannot be valid for any purpose.

Placing a date on the preceding quotation would be an interesting exercise. Younger readers might guess that it came from the 1974 *Standards for Educational and Psychological Tests,* (American Psychological Association, 1974) or perhaps a current draft of the revision of those standards. Others might think that the language sounds somewhat like the Equal Employment Opportunity Commission (EEOC) guidelines, which have been in existence for eight years. Middle-aged readers would probably assign the quotation to a text in educational measurement which they read fifteen to twenty years ago.

Only the more senior readers, or an occasional history buff, would guess that it appeared in 1947, in *Construction and Analysis of Achievement Tests,* written by Dorothy C. Adkins (and sold by the U.S. Government Printing Office at a price of $1.25).

The subtitle of the book was *The Development of Written and Performance Tests of Achievement for Predicting Job Performance of Public Personnel.* The focus of Dr. Adkins's book was civil service examinations. The focus of this book is licensure examinations. Thirty-seven years have passed, and many changes have occurred in the measurement of achievement and performance. Some things have not changed. Validity is still of prime consideration; a good test must be reliable. And, as was true in 1947, a test with no reliability cannot be valid for any purpose.

The purpose of licensing is protection, as is well explicated elsewhere in this volume. The purpose of examining the reliability and validity of examinations used to make licensing decisions is also protection. The protection notions associated with validity and reliability of licensure examinations are bidirectional—that is, both the examinees and the public are the focus.

Relationship to Scores and Decisions

Before pursuing the discussion of reliability and validity, two points need to be made: (1) Examinations are neither reliable nor valid; *scores* from examinations may be reliably or validly interpreted. (2) Examination scores are used to make decisions;

the decisions may be reliable and/or valid. Note that it is possible for scores and decisions to be reliable without being valid.

The nature of the discussions of reliability and validity revolve around investigating the extent to which licensure examinations produce scores which can be interpreted reliably and validly and which lead to reliable and valid decisions. The decision, which is of primary concern, is the point around which the circle of protection for the public and for the examinee is drawn.

If a licensure examination produces scores which cannot be reliably interpreted, then unreliable decisions will result. What this means, operationally, is that if a potential licensee takes the same test on different occasions, different scores may result and different decisions may be made. Such fluctuations in scores result from random errors associated with either the examination itself, for example, ambiguous items, or with testing conditions, such as poor lighting, or with the examinee, for example, a headache. Virtually every examination suffers from some of this random error, but it can often be held to a minimum by carefully controlling the construction of the examination and testing conditions. When this random error is not adequately controlled, some qualified examinees may not be licensed while some unqualified examinees may be licensed. By enhancing reliability to its maximum, the qualified examinees receive more protection from failure due to circumstances beyond their control, and the public is protected because unqualified examinees are less likely to be licensed.

Random errors cannot, of course, be eliminated. However, there are strategies one can use to construct examinations, administer, and score them such that some causes of unreliability are reduced to a minimum. Most textbooks on test construction, such as Gronlund's (1981), provide guidelines for constructing and administering tests. These guidelines, when followed, tend to enhance the reliability of test scores.

Reliability of Scores

Having constructed an examination and planned its administration(s) using established guidelines, studies to assess the reliability of scores and decisions are necessary (Equal Employment Opportunity Commission and others, 1978). The American Psychological Association (APA) *Standards for Educational and Psychological Tests* (1974) provides guidelines for selecting the most appropriate methods for estimating the reliability of scores. Although reliability can be conceptualized in a variety of ways, for example, in terms of true scores or domain sampling, it is operationalized in terms of consistency of measurement and/or decisions.

Traditionally, there are three classes of consistency—stability, equivalence, and homogeneity. Underlying stability is the dimension of time—that is, given the same examination on two different occasions, will the scores be the same? Clearly, there are assumptions about intervening learning, memory, and so on associated with this concept of consistency. Equivalence relates to the use of two or more alternate forms of an examination, each of which may be substituted for the other yet provide the same score interpretation. There are various assumptions associated with the extent to which the multiple forms are parallel to each other. Homogeneity refers to the extent that the items within the examination are internally consistent with each other, and this concept represents a means of estimating the degree of relationship between the extant version of the test and some hypothetical, parallel version. The methods for estimating the reliability of scores entail using one or more of these notions of consistency.

Stability. Stability is estimated by administering one examination to the same group of persons on two separate occasions and computing the coefficient of correlation between the two sets of scores—this is called the test-retest method. The resulting correlation coefficient is reported as a reliability estimate. The group of examinees should be a representative sample from those individuals whose scores will be used to make licensing decisions. The time span between administrations should be fairly short—one to two weeks.

Equivalence. Equivalence is determined by administering the different test forms to the same group of individuals, typically using a counterbalanced design—that is, give Form A to one half of the group and Form B to the other half; then administer the two forms in reverse order later in the day. A coefficient of correlation is computed between the scores from the two forms. This coefficient is reported as an estimate of alternate-forms reliability. A short time span could intervene between the first test administration period and the second, thereby providing for estimates of both equivalence and stability. Clearly, the group should be a representative sample of those who will be licensed using either of the two forms.

Homogeneity. Homogeneity refers to the extent to which the items on the test are internally consistent. It can be estimated by subdividing the test into two equivalent halves, following administration, and computing the correlation coefficient between the scores on the two halves. This coefficient is an underestimate of the reliability of the scores and must be adjusted by using the Spearman-Brown prophecy formula (see, for example, Gronlund, 1981). The method of splitting the test into two equivalent sets of items may involve using judges to determine the two sets (American Psychological Association, 1974). Several methods are available to estimate the average of all possible split-half combinations. The most frequently used are KR-20 (Kuder and Richardson, 1937) for items scored either right or wrong or coefficient alpha (Cronbach, 1951) for other item types, for example, attitude scale items.

Coefficient alpha and KR-20 are equivalent to each other conceptually and represent estimates of the correlation between the measure under consideration and a hypothetical alternate (randomly parallel) form. The formulas for these reliability estimates are not given here because they are included in almost every basic measurement text and in many educational research methods texts.

Choosing the Method. Each type of reliability estimate emphasizes different sources of error: test-retest focuses on errors associated with memory (the extent to which examinees recall their previous answers) and learning from the examination; alternate-forms emphasizes the extent to which the items on both forms represent the same domain of content; and internal-consistency permits inferences about content equivalence of items. The reliability estimate derived from each of these methods is also affected by such things as ambiguity of directions or items, testing conditions, examinee emotional and physical conditions, test length, range of talent, guessing, and so on.

The choice of which method to use depends on several factors. If there is only one form of the examination, test-retest and internal-consistency estimates are possible and desirable. A second form will eventually be needed, for security reasons or because of changes in the field, and at that point some estimate of equivalence will be needed, if not as an estimate of reliability, then for purposes of equating. We recommend that the development of alternate forms be done early and that the development of new items be an ongoing and continuous process. Such items need not be scored and used in making the licensing decision, but rather can be "banked" for use in later examinations. The Educational Testing Service and other test developers use this strategy, and their procedures manuals can offer insights on techniques.

For virtually every examination, coefficient alpha or KR-20 should be calculated. The exception is when there is a speed factor. A speed factor occurs when some items are not reached by a large number of examinees because of restrictive time limits or when the test is designed to measure the speed of performance, and errors will be random and not generally because of lack of knowledge.

The above methods for estimating the reliability of scores will provide a number which reflects, for the group taking the examination, a measure of the random error associated with the examination $(1.0 - r_{tt})$, where r_{tt} is the reliability estimate. However, these estimates will not be sufficient. The standard error of measurement (especially the error at the cut score) and assessment of the reliability of the decision may be needed. In addition, such things as the reliability of scorers or raters in either the predictor or criterion component may be required if there is a subjective element in the examination process.

Error of Measurement. The standard error of measurement is typically more stable than the reliability estimate (American Psychological Association, 1974). The reliability estimate can fluctuate across different samples of individuals, while the error of measurement will not fluctuate as widely.[1] The error of measurement is the statistic of choice for interpreting individual scores, hence becoming relevant in licensure examinations which clearly involve individual decisions.

The error of measurement is, theoretically, constant throughout the distribution of scores. However, theory takes a back seat to reality because the error of measurement varies—it becomes larger at the extremes of the score distribution and smaller at the mean. The effects of this variability in the error of measurement are most relevant for scores at or near the cut score, the score below which examinees are not licensed. It is clearly desirable to construct a licensing examination which has high reliability overall, but most particularly around the cut score. Although setting cut scores will be discussed in following sections, one method of achieving this goal is to design the test such that the average score (the mean) and the cut score coincide.[2]

Decision Reliability

Having constructed an examination, administered and scored it, set a cut score, and estimated the reliability and the realiability of scores around the cut score, it is now possible to estimate decision reliability. The method used to accomplish this will depend on whether the examination was administered to the same group on only one occasion or if a test-retest or an

[1] For example, suppose one sample had a wide range of talent which resulted in a reliability estimate of .96 and standard deviation of 10 score points. The error of measurement would be $s_m = s_y / 1 - r_{tt} = 10/1 - .96 = 2.0$. Another sample of examinees may be more homogeneous, resulting in a test standard deviation of 5 and a reduced reliability estimate of .86, which still results in a measurement error of 2.0. Note that each of the methods of estimating reliability involves using score variances—the lower the score variance, the lower the reliability estimate. This does not mean that the test is really unreliable, although that is one explanation. It could mean that the numeric index used may be suppressed and hence the reliability is underestimated.

[2] This strategy does not mean that only one half of the examinees will pass the test. The distribution of scores may be skewed, hence more (or fewer) than half may pass.

alternate-forms procedure was used. Estimating the reliability of the decision when only one score is available entails using one of several techniques summarized by Linn (1979). The techniques involve estimation of the consistency of the decisions and are based either on kappa (Cohen, 1960) or on estimating an unadjusted coefficient of agreement. The kappa-based method was developed by Huynh (1976), while the coefficient of agreement estimate is attributed by Linn to Subkoviak (1976).

The Huynh model requires complex calculations, although an approximation procedure can be used when the examination has more than ten items, as would be the case in most licensure examinations. The number produced by this method has a value between 0.0 and +1.0 and represents an index of the extent of decision agreement based on scores from the test administered and a hypothetical parallel form. The magnitude of the estimate is not test-specific, however, as it depends on the cut score, test length, and variability. Specifically, "kappa tends to be lower for criterion scores near the extremes, to increase with test length, and to increase with test variability" (Linn, 1979, p. 100). Thus, if Huynh's approach is used and the resulting kappa reported, it would also be essential to describe the testing situation and the cut score (Linn, 1979).

Subkoviak's approach appears to be simpler than Huynh's. It involves selecting one of two methods for estimating each individual's true score and then estimating the probability that the true score is above or below the cut score on the actual test and on a hypothetical parallel test. Like kappa, the resulting coefficient of agreement depends on the cut score. Unlike kappa, higher proportions of agreement were obtained when cut scores were near the extremes than for intermediate values (Linn, 1979). In an empirical investigation, Subkoviak found that this model slightly underestimated the index of agreement obtained when the measures were administered on two occasions, but the amount of underestimation was not serious.

Clearly, the determination of decision consistency is best accomplished by using two administrations of the measure. Linn also reviews several of these procedures. For licensure examinations the use of kappa (Cohen, 1960) would represent our method of choice for estimating the degree of decision consistency. In essence, kappa represents the corrected-for-chance proportion of agreement of assignment to nominal categories of pass/fail given two independent test administrations for the same group. As an example, suppose two administrations of a licensure examination result in the classifications shown in Table 1.

Table 1. Classifications Resulting from Two Administrations of a Licensure Examination.

Second Administration of Test	First Administration of Test: License	First Administration of Test: Fail to license	
License	.80	.05	.85
Fail to license	.10	.05	.15
	.90	.10	1.00

In this illustration, 80 percent of the applicants would be licensed based on their scores from both administrations, while 5 percent would not be licensed by both exams. The proportion of agreement would be

$$p_o = .80 + .05 = .85$$

Using the marginal totals, the proportion of agreement expected by chance would be

$$p_c = (.90)(.85) + (.10)(.15) = .78$$

Kappa, then, is the proportion of agreement corrected for chance.

$$k = \frac{p_o - p_c}{1 - p_c} = \frac{.85 - .78}{1 - .78} = .32$$

As kappa approaches 1.00 it reflects greater agreement; a kappa of zero represents agreement explained only by chance, while negative values would indicate a systematic bias reflecting less than chance agreement. Huynh (1976) argues that negative values of kappa are not logically interpretable. As the cut score diverges from the mean score into the more error-prone extremes, kappa will be reduced. An advantage of using kappa is that it can be applied when more than two decision categories are used. Suppose, for example, that a licensure procedure permitted multiple, progressive steps such that passing the first stage was required before the second could be entered. To protect individuals from too early a rejection, a borderline category, for example, scores plus or minus two standard errors of measurement around the cut score, could be added to the categories of passing and failing. Such a strategy would result in protecting those who were incorrectly classified as failing by giving them a second chance and would protect the public by decreasing the chances that an unqualified applicant would pass the second hurdle.

Complicating Factors in Reliability Estimates

Multipart Tests. Up to now we have discussed reliability of scores and decisions as though the licensure examination resulted in a single score that was used to make the licensing decision. In some cases this does not occur. Many licensure examinations are really test batteries consisting of two or more tests, each covering a different topic. For example, Menges (1975) reports that the pharmacy licensing examination is a two-part examination: a written part covering theory and a "practice of pharmacy" section. In some cases the licensing decision might rest on whether or not candidates passed each part (as in the pharmacy examination), or the decision could be made on the basis of a total (combined) score. The estimation of the reliability of scores from a test containing several parts or content areas is complex, since both coefficient alpha and KR-20 assume that the test is unidimensional, that is, measuring only one topical area. A test-retest reliability estimate would, therefore, be desirable. When this is not possible, the reliability of the total score can be estimated using a procedure described by Nunnally (1978). The formula is

$$r_{tt} = 1 - \frac{\Sigma\sigma_i^2 - \Sigma r_{ii}\,\sigma_i^2}{\sigma_t^2}$$

where r_{tt} = total score reliability
σ_i^2 = variance of the ith subtest
r_{ii} = subtest reliability
σ_t^2 = total score variance

To our knowledge, no similar combinatorial method has been developed to estimate decision reliability. Linn (1979) described two studies which indicated that tests with high (low) internal consistency reliability tended to have high (low) kappas. Thus, if the total score reliability using the above formula is high, Huynh's (1976) simplified estimate of decision reliability may be adequate, although likely an underestimate, as an approximation of kappa.

Human Judgment Factors. A more complex reliability problem than combining scores across subtests arises when the licensure examination involves other than multiple-choice or similar types of items. Specifically, when human judgment is a factor in arriving at the score used in making the licensure decision, reliability is likely to be reduced. This problem, however, should not be viewed as our advocating that the tail (reliability) wag the dog (validity). If, in order to achieve fidelity, scoring must be done by observations/ratings, which are less reliable than multiple-choice items, then it is incumbent on the licensing agency to ensure the thorough training of scorers and to take such other steps as may be necessary to increase interrater consistency.

Norm- or Criterion-Referenced Tests. In the preceding discussion of reliability we have not distinguished between norm-referenced and criterion-referenced tests. Elsewhere in this book it is stated that licensure examinations are criterion-referenced. Technically, it is the score interpretation, not the examination, that is either norm- or criterion-referenced. Hence, the discussion of reliability incorporates the fundamental notions of either type of score interpretation. Specifically, when the reliability of the score itself is of interest, a norm-referenced interpretation is assumed; when the score is reduced to decision categories based on its relationship to a cut score, the interpretation is criterion-referenced and the reliability of the decision is of interest. Note that the decision represents a score of either 0 (failing) or 1 (passing). The same notions apply to certain of the validity concepts discussed in the following section.

Disagreement on Requirements for Validity Evidence

Considerable disagreement exists among experts about the extensiveness of validity evidence needed for licensure examinations. Shimberg (1981) and Kane (1982) suggest that content validation is sufficient, while Hecht (1979) argues that, in addition to content validation, evidence of criterion-related validity (job-related performance being the criterion) is also needed.

Few authors argue in support of construct validation studies, and none were found that referenced instructional and curricular validity (McClung, 1978). Yalow and Popham (1983) suggest that concerns about instructional and curriculum content may not be validity issues in the psychometric sense even though such concerns are relevant to ensure a fair examination which can pass certain legal challenges. Recent validation studies of the National Teacher Examinations in states which use this as a certification examination have been concerned with instructional and curriculum content as a means of defining the content domain (see Cross, 1982, for example). (Although called certification, the use of the examination is consistent with the notion of licensure, that is, as an entry-level screening device to protect the public.)

Cronbach (1983) argues that construct validity should be of concern as a basis for deciding what is worth testing. Construct validity evidence, in addition to evidence supporting the other concepts of validity, is needed to support complete interpretations of most scores (American Educational Research Association, 1983).

The federal guidelines (Equal Employment Opportunity Commission and others, 1978) are frequently considered as one legal authority on validity. The applicability of these guidelines to licensure is unclear, except that to the extent that licensure is or may be construed as discriminatory the guidelines apply. These guidelines parallel the APA *Standards for Educational and Psychological Tests* (1974) in defining validity concepts and in discussing which aspect of validity is appropriate. The crux of the argument is that the appropriate validity depends upon the intended use of the scores. These 1974 standards are in the process of being revised, and the revision is expected to be published in 1985. The revised standards will include a section devoted specifically to licensure examinations. The thrust of this chapter does not conflict with the draft of the revised standards made available during this writing (American Education Research Association, American Psychological Association, and National Council on Measurement in Education, 1983); however, the reader who is involved in either constructing or using licensure examinations should certainly obtain from the APA a copy of the revised standards as soon as they become available. We tend to concur with Shimberg and Kane that the validation focus for licensure examinations is content validity, and with Cross, Kane, and others that when specialized training is a requisite for licensure, some attention to instructional content is also relevant. However, our agreement with these positions does not go so far as to exclude discussion of strategies for criterion-related and construct validation studies.

Validation Terms and Concepts

At this point, some definitions are in order.

- *Content validation* is "the procedure by which the content of a test is judged to be representative of some universe of content" (American Psychological Association, 1983, pp. 2-3).
- *Criterion-related validation* is the extent to which

scores on "the test predict scores on a well-specified *criterion.* In this context the criterion is the variable of primary interest" (American Educational Research Association, 1983, pp. 2-6, emphasis in original).

- *Construct validation* is the process by which scores from a set of measurement operations are given interpretation or meaning which should be embedded in a conceptual framework (American Educational Research Association, 1983, pp. 2-4).
- *Curricular validity* "is a measure of how well test items represent the objectives of the curriculum" (McClung, 1978, p. 397).
- *Instructional validity* "is an actual measure of whether the schools are providing students with instruction in the knowledge and skills measured by the test" (McClung, 1978, p. 397).

The mechanics of assessing content, instructional, and curriculum validity often have several similar components. The components of these three validity concepts will be discussed first, followed by criterion-related and construct validity.

Content Validity. Perhaps if the notion of protection is again raised, the logic of validation strategies will be made clear. To ensure that the public will be protected from incompetent licensees (note that the licensure examination will not protect the public from a competent but unscrupulous licensee, as the examination is not given from a morality perspective), the job to be performed must be examined critically to assess those job components which if not performed competently may result in harm to the public. For example, a nuclear power plant operator who cannot recognize a critical emergency, or a physician who prescribes a contraindicated medication, or an accountant who is unfamiliar with the tax code would be hazardous and should not be licensed. However, a real estate salesman who is a bore or a physician unaware of the tax advantages of incorporation may be licensed since these characteristics are not part of the required professional knowledge. (The salesman and doctor may not, however, be "successful.")

A thorough job analysis which differentiates "protection"

tasks from those tasks needed to be "successful" is essential. Such tasks must be further analyzed to ascertain the specific knowledge and/or skills necessary for task accomplishment. Typically, the knowledges/skills, or a sample of them, are included on the licensure examination. It is argued (Kane, 1982; Shimberg, 1981) that the knowledges/skills are all that should be included.

How is such a task analysis performed? Kane (1982) suggests that "critical abilities" may be ascertained empirically or through logical analysis. Certain aspects of professions which are subject to licensure entail a general set of knowledge/skills which can be delineated through observation of persons involved in the profession, for example, pharmacists preparing prescriptions or nurses giving injections. In other aspects of the profession, the occurrence of certain incidents (such as adverse reaction to medication) is rare, hence it may be unlikely to observe them in the course of empirical job analysis.

Activities which are relatively common and observable can be detected through job analysis by watching professionals work. Other activities must be ascertained through extensive interviews with experienced professionals. During such interviews the analyst confirms the criticality of essential tasks noted during observation.

Another part of job analysis involves the identification of knowledge and skills associated with the task, the assignment of appropriate weights to them, and the selection of those to be measured. The original job analysis will likely result in a long list of knowledge, skills, and behaviors that are related to safe practice. For many fields, the list will be too lengthy for comprehensive measurement. Some strategy must be employed to reduce the list. One such strategy involves assigning weights to each knowledge, skill, and behavior component. There are many ways to assign weights—empirical time analysis, studies requiring professional logs, critical incidents techniques, expert judgment, or some combination of these ways (Kane, 1982).

The job analysis and subsequent selection of examination content are the critical steps in determining content validity. There is no direct mathematical or statistical index of content validity; rather, content validity is a judgmental process. Certain statistical indices can provide useful information in support of content validity, for example, internal consistency reliability and factor analysis. However, these procedures alone are not sufficient.

Curricular and Instructional Validity. Curricular and instructional validity evidence may be inferred using such strategies as accreditation. Validity evidence can also be sought by examining course syllabi (curricular validity) or by obtaining samples of classroom tests or conducting classroom observations (instructional validity). While neither of these validity concepts has been employed specifically as a validation strategy, these and other methods are used to help ensure that the contents of licensure examinations incorporate samples of essential knowledge and skills which are taught in training programs.

Criterion-Related Validation. Criterion-related validation is, on the surface, a straightforward mathematical procedure that involves correlating scores on a test with scores on some criterion measure. The difficult part is defining the criterion. Clearly, any criterion measure must also be one which is valid. But for a licensure decision, what represents a valid criterion measure? If the purpose of licensure is public protection, one might suppose that the criterion would be some measure of practitioner "errors" that result in client harm. However, if the licensure examination does its job of screening out applicants who are not knowledgeable and/or skillful, then so few errors will occur that the correlation will be virtually meaningless (due to restriction of range on the criterion variable scores). Even if a measure of errors was a workable criterion, when should the measure be taken—during the first few months after licensure, between one and five years later, or at some other time? In what setting should the criterion measure be taken? For some professions there may be sufficient similarity across settings to make this question inappropriate, but for other professions the setting makes a considerable difference in the nature of the work and the nature of client contact.

Hecht (1979) argues strongly in support of criterion-related validation. She suggests that the criterion should be a measure of job-related performance. While such a measure may be useful as a substitute for or adjunct to multiple-choice or other traditional testing methods, it does not resolve the problems of setting, timing, or restricted ranges of scores noted earlier. She correctly points out, however, that there is seldom much of a relationship between measures of knowledge and skills and measures of actual performance. Individuals who respond correctly to questions about knowledge and skills may or may not perform in a knowledgeable or skillful way in actual practice. Her suggestion about using a measure of job-related performance, as is done in the pharmacy examination, has considerable merit. But such a measure is a component of the licensure process, hence it is not a criterion measure in the psychometric sense.

We were unable to locate any systematic criterion-related validation studies of licensure examinations. There were studies which used the licensure examination as a criterion measure, but none which used the licensure examination as the "predictor." Clearly, then, topics in need of future investigation are defining appropriate criterion measures for licensure examinations and, having such criterion measures, estimating criterion-related validity.

Construct Validation. Construct validation is discussed extensively in the 1974 and revised APA standards mentioned previously. In the 1983 draft standards, six types of evidence which may contribute to construct interpretations are presented. Of these, most seem relevant to licensure examinations. All rely on clear definitions of the construct and a conceptual framework associated with the construct. The six types of evidence include (American Educational Research Association, American Psychological Association, and National Council on Measurement in Education, 1983):

- Interitem correlation: If the measure relates to a single, unified construct, then items measuring the construct should have high intercorrelations.
- Intervariable correlation: If the theory or conceptual

framework suggests relationships of the construct being measured with some constructs but not with others, then the measure should correlate more highly with measures of related constructs than with unrelated constructs. Such measures need not be tests; they may also be educational or occupational background measures.

- Intermeasure correlation: If aspects of the measurement process can introduce bias or error, such a possibility should be ruled out or accounted for by correlating scores from measures of different content which rely on the same measurement process. For example, multiple-choice tests of law knowledge should correlate more highly with each other than with multiple-choice tests of accounting procedures.
- Interjudge correlation: Content and construct validation "overlap when experts are asked to judge the adequacy of the methods used to sample item content from the universe of content and the adequacy with which the measurement operations seem to reflect the theoretical definitions of the construct" (pp. 2–6).
- Interindividual correlation: Interviews with individual respondents or raters about the processes they used to respond to specific items should reveal similar processes, and these processes should be related to the construct.
- Criterion-predictor intercorrelation: If an inappropriate criterion measure is used, spurious intercorrelation may result due to contamination by an irrelevant variable, for example, both the predictor and criterion measures having high verbal components when the job in question does not require high verbal skills.

To the extent that licensure examinations can be construed to be measures of theoretically based constructs, these and other strategies of providing evidence of construct validity are appropriate. It seems that this determination of appropriateness applies to almost all such examinations. Our logic is that there is at least an implicit conceptual relationship between the test content and "safe" practice. To the extent that such connections cannot be made, the test content may not be appropriate for licensure.

Explicit conceptual connections between test content and safe practice may not be sufficient, however. There are many studies showing low correlations between knowledge and practice. Such evidence argues strongly that, to the extent possible, a practice component be included as a part of the licensure examination.

In some cases the primary evidence of construct validation is only implied through the assurance that a licensure applicant has matriculated from an accredited institution. Hence, possession of knowledge, skills, and other essential attributes is assumed (Shimberg, 1981). This practice, while it clearly has shortcomings, may have to suffice for fields where explicit measurement of all attributes needed to ensure competence would be impossible or impractical.

Validity of Cut Scores and Decisions

The three components of validity of scores—content, criterion-related, and construct—relate to the direct interpretation of scores; they relate to the extent to which inferences about knowledge, skills, and practice may be validly made from scores on the licensure examination. In addition to these inferences, licensure requires an inference about competence. Specifically, the examination score should provide an inference about specific knowledges and skills, while the licensure decision provides an inference about sufficiency of competence.

A licensure decision can also be considered a score: zero for those deemed incompetent and one for those who "pass." It is this notion that was the basis for discussing the reliability of the decision. This same concept is considered in some methods of assessing the validity of the decision. However, the mathematics of assessing the validity of the cut score, when it can be undertaken mathematically, are much simpler than the conceptual interpretation.

The qualitative meaning of minimal competence is often difficult to fathom, and linking the meaning to a score on an examination is equally perplexing. Because of this difficulty, the validation of the resulting decision has resulted in much more rhetoric than has the more technical issue, reliability.

In its brief history, discussions about methods of setting cut scores have resulted in at least two points of agreement: (1) Setting cut scores involves judgment at some point in the process. (2) Different methods will result in different scores, which may show wide variation in the number of examinees who pass.

It is the latter point which is the most problematic. If the same (or a randomly equivalent) group of judges uses two different methods to set a score on a given test such that individuals who score above that point are declared competent, why do different score points occur? Do the judges' notions of minimal competence differ? Clearly, much research is still needed in the area of validation of cut scores.

In the meantime, decisions about licensure must still be made. Such decisions may rely on cut scores set using a normative base—for example, the highest-scoring 20 percent may pass, without regard to how high or low their scores are, or an absolute score base may be used such that all examinees who can answer 75 percent of the questions on the examination will be considered to have entry-level knowledge and skills. In professions where there is an appropriate criterion related to the protection concept of licensure, information from the validation study may aid in setting the cut score. There are many methods of setting cut scores within these two broad classifications. These methods are reviewed by such authors as Hambleton, 1980; Livingston and Zieky, 1982; and Shepard, 1980. There is no clear agreement on the single best method for setting cut scores. We are of the opinion that all of the methods have fundamental flaws, but we are unable to argue for an alternative to the present approaches. It is clearly essential that the method used in a particular licensure situation be described in detail, along with the rationale for selecting the particular strategy used.

References

Adkins, D. C. *Construction and Analysis of Achievement Tests: The Development of Written and Performance Tests of Achievement for Predicting Job Performance of Public Per-*

sonnel. Washington, D.C.: U.S. Government Printing Office, 1947.

American Educational Research Association, American Psychological Association, and National Council on Measurement in Education. *Draft Joint Technical Standards for Educational and Psychological Testing.* Washington, D.C.: American Educational Research Association, 1983.

American Psychological Association, American Educational Research Association, and National Council on Measurement in Education. *Standards for Educational and Psychological Tests.* Washington, D.C.: American Psychological Association, 1974.

Cohen, J. A. "A Coefficient of Agreement for Nominal Scales." *Educational and Psychological Measurement,* 1960, *20,* 37-46.

Cronbach, L. J. "Coefficient Alpha and the Internal Structure of Tests." *Psychometrika,* 1951, *16,* 297-334.

Cronbach, L. J. "What Price Simplicity?" *Educational Measurement Issues and Practice,* 1983, *2,* 11-12.

Cross, L. *Final Report Validation Study of the National Teacher Examinations for Certification of Entry-Level Teachers in the State of Virginia, Phase I.* Richmond, Va.: Department of Education, 1982.

Equal Employment Opportunity Commission and others. "Adoption by Four Agencies of Uniform Guidelines on Employment Selection Procedures." *Federal Register,* 1978, *43,* 38290-38315.

Gronlund, N. E. *Measurement and Evaluation in Teaching.* (4th ed.) New York: Macmillan, 1981.

Hambleton, R. K. "Test Score Validity and Standard-Setting Methods." In R. A. Berk (Ed.) *Criterion-Referenced Measurement: The State of the Art.* Baltimore, Md.: Johns Hopkins University Press, 1980.

Hecht, K. A. "Current Status and Methodological Problems of Validating Professional Licensing and Certification Exams." In M. A. Bunda and J. R. Sanders (Eds.), *Practices and Problems in Competency-Based Education.* Washington, D.C.: National Council on Measurement in Education, 1979.

Huynh, H. "On the Reliability of Decisions in Domain-Referenced Testing." *Journal of Educational Measurement,* 1976, *13,* 253-264.

Kane, M. T. "The Validity of Licensure Examinations." *American Psychologist,* 1982, *37,* 911-918.

Kuder, G. F., and Richardson, M. W. "The Theory of the Estimation of Test Reliability." *Psychometrika,* 1937, *2,* 151-160.

Linn, R. L. "Issues of Reliability in Measurement for Competency-Based Programs." In M. A. Bunda and J. R. Sanders (Eds.), *Practices and Problems in Competency-Based Education.* Washington, D.C.: National Council on Measurement in Education, 1979.

Livingston, S. A., and Zieky, M. J. Passing Scores: A Manual for Setting Standards of Performance on Educational and Occupational Tests. Princeton, N.J.: Educational Testing Service, 1982.

McClung, M. S. "Are Competency Testing Programs Fair? Legal?" *Phi Delta Kappan,* 1978, *59,* 397-400.

Menges, R. J. "Assessing Readiness for Professional Practice." *Review of Educational Research,* 1975, *45,* 172-203.

Nunnally, J. C. *Psychometric Theory.* (2nd ed.) New York: McGraw-Hill, 1978.

Shepard, L. "Standard-Setting Issues and Methods." *Applied Psychological Measurement,* 1980, *4,* 447-467.

Shimberg, B. "Testing for Licensure and Certification." *American Psychologist,* 1981, *36,* 1138-1146.

Subkoviak, M. "Estimating Reliability from a Single Administration of a Criterion-Referenced Test." *Journal of Educational Measurement,* 1976, *13,* 265-276.

Yalow, E. S., and Popham, W. J. "Content Validity at the Crossroads." *Educational Researcher,* 1983, *12,* 10-14, 21.

5

Legal Issues in Licensing

Virginia C. Vertiz

This chapter provides an overview of the legal issues involved in occupational licensing. The chapter sections explore historical perspective, the power to license, licensing requirements and the law, examinations, and other legal issues. Litigation in both state and federal courts is discussed. Members of licensing boards may consider that litigation when establishing guidelines for regulating occupations.

Historical Perspective

In colonial times the learned professions were theology, medicine, and law (Gellhorn, 1976). For many years, with few exceptions, only medicine and law were licensed (Bradley, 1977). Most licensing laws are similar in content to those that govern medical and legal professions, as they were modeled after them. The licensing of occupations was an extension of the medieval guild system (Smith, 1982). Since the beginning of this century, a tremendous amount of legislation has been enacted, resulting in extensive licensing of occupations (Bradley, 1977). Today there are approximately 800 occupations regulated by state governments in the United States (Shimberg, 1981).

Power to License

The power to license occupations is derived from the United States Constitution and the constitutions of various states (Bradley, 1977). This power is the police power in American constitutional law—the reserved or inherent power of the states to provide for the protection of public health, safety, and general welfare. The Fourteenth Amendment states, in part, "No state shall make or enforce any law which shall abridge the privileges or immunities of citizens of the United States; nor shall any State deprive any person of life, liberty, or property without due process of law, nor deny to any person within its jurisdiction the equal protection of the laws."

The concept of police power evolved from the interpretation of the Fourteenth Amendment by the Supreme Court. "Licensing restrictions have generally been found to be a valid exercise of the state's police power" (Cathcart and Graff, 1978, p. 150). However, occupational licensing statutes are not immune to review under the amendment's due process clause. In order for the due process clause to apply, it must be shown that freedom to practice a certain occupation is a "liberty" or constitutes a "property" (Cathcart and Graff, 1978).

Though few cases concerning occupational licensing have been reviewed on due process grounds in federal courts, the due process clause can be used by both federal and state courts to review licensing statutes. Cathcart and Graff discuss three requirements that the due process clause makes on occupational licensing. "The licensing schemes must be drawn up with specificity, rationality, and fairness" (1978, p. 153).

Specificity refers to the standards by which a licensing board grants, denies, suspends, renews, or revokes a license. These guidelines must be understandable. Rationality means that those standards have some reasonable relationship to the practice of the licensed occupation. Fairness refers to the composition of the licensing board, its procedures, and the "necessity and timing of judicial review" (Cathcart and Graff, 1978, p. 153).

Fourteenth Amendment. Several Supreme Court decisions address the applicability of the Fourteenth Amendment to the licensing of occupations. In the 1884 decision of *Butchers' Union* v. *Crescent City Co.,* Justice Bradley ruled that the right to follow any of the occupations is an inalienable right (Howard, 1978). However, in 1954, the Court decision in *Barsky* v. *Board of Regents* held that freedom of occupational choice was not protected by the Fourteenth Amendment. The reasoning was that the practice of a certain occupation was deemed a privilege, rather than a right. More recently, the distinction between privilege and right has not been made. In *Schware* v. *Board of Bar Examiners* (1957) the Court made it clear that the due process and equal protection clauses of the Fourteenth Amendment are applicable to the freedom of occupational choice. Further stating that it was not necessary to discuss the distinction between right and privilege, the Court said that a person cannot be prevented from practicing except for valid reasons (Cathcart and Graff, 1978).

Freedom of occupational choice has also been regarded as a liberty and as such is protected by the Fourteenth Amendment. In both *Meyer* v. *Nebraska* (1923) and *Board of Regents* v. *Roth* (1972), the Court regarded freedom of occupational choice in this way, thereby creating a broad definition within the Fourteenth Amendment (Cathcart and Graff, 1978).

Although Justice Peckman's 1905 Supreme Court decision in *Lockner* v. *New York* implied that licensing was acceptable only for the professions (Howard, 1978), licensing has obviously become considerably more extensive. Beekeepers, embalmers, lightning rod salesmen, septic tank cleaners, taxidermists, and tree surgeons are among the nonprofessional callings now requiring licenses (Gellhorn, 1976).

In recent years the Supreme Court has refused to scrutinize licensing legislation closely (Howard, 1978). It has not, however, prevented the lower federal courts from using due process grounds to review occupational licensing statutes. In *Williamson* v. *Lee Optical, Inc.* (1955), the Supreme Court upheld a state statute that prevented opticians from making lenses without an optometrist's or ophthalmologist's prescription. The Court went on to declare that it did not intend to strike down state regulatory laws on due process grounds any longer (Cathcart and Graff, 1978).

Antitrust Laws. Perhaps because of its disdain of substantive due process, the Court has used antitrust laws to challenge state regulation (Gellhorn, 1976). Section 1 of the Sherman Act prohibits price-fixing and the potentially anticompetitive effects of occupational licensing. In 1943, the Supreme Court said that "the states should be free to make their own economic principles in vogue with the federal judiciary" (Gellhorn, 1976, p. 19).

Johnson and Corgel (1983) trace the history of the professional defense, which has evolved over the past sixty years. The Court, in distinguishing professions from other occupations, has granted antitrust immunity to members of the learned professions. In 1922, the Supreme Court found for the defense in *Federal Baseball Club* v. *National League.* Eight baseball clubs challenged the monopoly over major league baseball by two baseball leagues. The Court dismissed the antitrust challenge on jurisdictional grounds.

The second phase of the evolution of the professionalism defense is illustrated in *American Medical Association* v. *United States.* This 1943 case found against the American Medical Association (AMA) and the Medical Society of the District of Columbia on antitrust grounds. The defendants were charged with impeding a nonprofit group of government employees from setting up its own health plan. The purpose and effect of their action was to restrain competition for health insurance, so the jurisdictional defense was dismissed. Likewise, the Court found against the defendants in *United States* v. *National Association of Real Estate Boards* in 1950. Although also claiming a jurisdictional defense, the real estate board was accused of price-fixing.

In phase three, the Court began to make the distinction between professions and other occupations. The learned professions thereby became immune to the Sherman Act's restrictions. The *United States* v. *Oregon Medical Society* is cited to illustrate this point (Johnson and Corgel, 1983). Howard cites *People* v. *Beattie,* a 1904 case invalidating a state statute in Alabama requiring the licensing of horseshoers. The occupation was regarded as one of the most common, and unrelated to the health, safety, or welfare of society (1978).

Phase four rearticulated the "Rule of Reason" set forth in *Standard Oil Co.* v. *United States* in 1911. "According to this criterion, only when an occupational licensing scheme exerts a net procompetitive effect on the price and quality of professional services offered for sale should it be granted immunity from the Sherman Act" (Johnson and Corgel, 1983, p. 485). Two more recent cases, *Goldfarb* v. *Virginia State Bar* of 1975 and the *National Society of Professional Engineers* v. *United States* (1978), justified price-fixing under the "Rule of Reason."

Licensing Requirements and the Law

The state courts have continued to review occupational licensing statutes in terms of their validity, even though the Supreme Court has not (Cathcart and Graff, 1978). A variety of requirements has been imposed on the licensing process. These requirements concern, among other issues, imposition of a fee, bonding, certain personal qualifications, recommendations, education and training, apprenticeships, experience, and examinations (Howard, 1978; Cathcart and Graff, 1978). The validity of these requirements has been discussed on a number of legal bases. Title VII of the Civil Rights Act of 1964, an employment antidiscrimination statute, appears not to apply to state licensing, according to the few federal circuit courts of appeal that have considered the issue (Shimberg, 1981).

There is some question as to whether or not the federal "Uniform Guidelines on Employee Selection Procedures" of 1978, sponsored by the Equal Employment Opportunity Commission and other agencies, are applicable to licensing legislation. A number of federal courts of appeal decisions including *Tyler* v. *Vickery* (1975), *Parrish* v. *Board of Commissioners of Alabama State Bar* (1976), and *Richardson* v. *McFadden* (1976) held that state licensing activities are not employment practices (Science Management Corporation, 1982). The Uniform Guidelines are usually applied only when discrimination in employment is claimed under Title VII and where a prima facie, or "self-evident," case of discrimination is established. Since Title VII is considered inapplicable, the Uniform Guidelines must be as well.

Two federal court decisions, *Puntilillo* v. *New Hampshire*

Racing Commission (1975) and *Sibley Memorial* v. *Wilson* (1973) seem to indicate that the Uniform Guidelines do apply to licensing. Because the facts of these cases did not involve issues of employee competence, they do not necessarily contradict the federal courts of appeal decisions (Science Management Corporation, 1982).

"The Uniform Guidelines state that the 'user' of a selection procedure has the responsibility for its validation" (Science Management Corporation, 1982, p. 18). The question of whether the "user" is the employer where licensing is involved is still unclear. Although the Science Management Corporation (1982) claims the issue is unresolved, Shimberg (1981) cites Section 5 of the General Principles of the Uniform Guidelines, which says, "If an employer relies upon such certification in making employment decisions, the employer is the user and must be prepared to justify, under federal law, that reliance as it would any other selection procedure."

The Supreme Court has made no decisions on these questions. However, a number of authors suggest that licensing procedures, including examinations, meet certain standards of validity that are performance-oriented rather than attribute-oriented (Science Management Corporation, 1982). A discussion of validity issues as they pertain to the various procedures follows.

License Fees. In Alabama the cost of a license imposed under police power may not exceed the cost of its issuance plus a reasonable amount for supervision of that occupation. Reasonable supervision costs of municipal licensing include expenses associated with disorders, fires, sanitation, and other safety functions. Reasonable supervision costs of legislatively created licensing include expenses involved with testing, licensing, board meetings, investigatory activities, quasi-judicial activities, and litigation (Howard, 1978).

Bonds. The reasonableness of the amount of the bond would be the basis for challenge to this licensing requirement. In *People* v. *Masters* (1971), an Illinois case, the court invalidated a statute requiring plumbers to pay a $125 license fee and post a $20,000 bond, saying that the requirements bore no relationship to the public health (Howard, 1978).

Personal Qualifications. Individuals are variously restricted from entry into licensed occupations by having to meet personal qualifications. Among these are citizenship, residency, character, age, and race requirements (Rose, 1979; Howard, 1978; Voigt, 1980).

Requirements of citizenship are probably unconstitutional. In 1976 the Supreme Court held that an applicant to practice as a civil engineer cannot be denied a license because he is a noncitizen in *Examining Board of Engineers, Architects, and Surveyors* v. *Florez de Otero*. Likewise, due process was deemed violated in *Hampton* v. *Mow Dun Wong* (1976) when a noncitizen was denied entrance into a federal competitive civil service position. Cases concerning aliens' admission to the bar have been tried on a state-by-state basis. In each instance, the court has found for the defendant. (Examples of this litigation include *Sheley* v. *Alaska Bar Association* of 1980, *Gordon* v. *Committee on Character and Fitness* of 1980, and *In re Griffiths* of 1973.) The validity of statutes requiring citizenship must be challenged by the license applicants themselves (Gellhorn, 1976).

Residency requirements are also attached to occupational licensing guidelines. Although it would seem that optometrists, accountants, masseurs, and dentists would perform the same services from state to state, the statutes "pretend that one must have lived within the license-issuing state in order to understand its citizenry's needs" (Gellhorn, 1976, p. 15). Some states even allow counties and cities to make occupational licensing contingent upon local residence. Auctioneers, plumbers, lawn-sprinkler installers, stationary engineers, and fortune tellers are barred from practicing locally without local experience (Gellhorn, 1976).

Another personal qualification, good moral character, has been criticized because it is almost impossible to test (Howard, 1978). "In some states, virtually the only 'profession' open to a once-convicted felon is that of burglar; he is barred from other activities because he is presumed to be a person of bad moral character, regardless of the nature of the felony or its relevance to his intended occupation" (Gellhorn, 1976).

Attempts have been made to deny applicants admission

to the bar based on sexual conduct. In Florida a 1978 decision in *Re Florida Board of Bar Examiners* "held that an applicant to the state bar except insofar as his acknowledged homosexuality precluded his establishing his good moral character, would be admitted to the bar" (Miller, 1983, p. 1110). In *Spears* v. *State Bar of California* (1931) the court held that an applicant's moral character was in question, as he had been charged with interstate transportation of women for prostitution. (Further discussion of cases relevant to sexual conduct as it affects admission to the bar can be found in Miller, 1983.)

Cases involving eligibility for or restoration of a license as affected by a pardon are discussed by Hall (1974). The general consensus is that a pardon does not result in the automatic restoration of a license forfeited because of a crime but, rather, that it opens the door for reconsideration of the qualifications of the applicant.

Certain age requirements are probably valid. Those statutes requiring real estate brokers or salespersons to have reached majority have been upheld. But in Arizona statutes requiring polygraph examiners to be twenty-five were struck down in 1935 in *City of Tucson* v. *Stewart* (Howard, 1978).

Personal requirements that have excluded a particular race have been held unconstitutional under the equal protection clause. In *Bell* v. *Georgia Dental Association* (1964) a statute limiting appointments of the Board of Dental Examiners to nominees of the Georgia Dental Association, which excluded blacks, was struck down (Voigt, 1980).

It appears that statutes requiring applicants for licenses to obtain recommendations from citizens are constitutional. However, in a case pending in Alabama, the supreme court has not yet ruled on the constitutionality of requiring recommendations from practitioners or employers. The legality of statutes requiring recommendations from property owners seems questionable (Howard, 1978).

Whether or not such statutes are constitutional, the behavior of an individual from one situation to the next is too inconsistent where moral judgment is concerned. Further, even if behavior could be predicted accurately, anyone can obtain recommendations from citizens or practitioners if the applicant knows them. And just because an applicant knows no practitioners or employers in the field does not mean that he or she is unsuited for the profession (Howard, 1978).

The requirement of obtaining employer recommendations is open to abuse. An employer could be considered an agent of the state when deciding whom to recommend and whom not to recommend. Procedural due process could prohibit arbitrary withholding of recommendations if other state actions indicated licensing (Howard, 1978).

Educational requirements have been upheld by Alabama courts except for the decision in *Barbers Commission* v. *Hardeman* (1945). Regarding barbering as a skilled trade, rather than a profession, the court said in *Hardeman* that it would not exclude a man from an ordinary occupation because of his lack of education. Currently, Alabama courts are not expected to rule according to *Hardeman* because of the change in technology since 1945 (Howard, 1978).

In California, graduation from a barber college is a requisite for entering the barbering profession. In Illinois, barbering hopefuls must pass tests in physiology, electricity, anatomy, and barber history (Gellhorn, 1976). Most states require "institutionalized instruction in bacteriology; histology of the hair, skin, nails, muscles, and nerves; diseases of the skin, hair, glands, and nails; and other matters about which one may venture to guess few barbers are consulted" (Gellhorn, 1976, p. 13). Although most barbering exams are based on a single small booklet, these Illinois educational requirements still prevail. The time and money necessary to meet those requirements restrict entry into the occupation to those willing to make the investment (Gellhorn, 1976).

Apprenticeships are sometimes required of an applicant for a license. In California an apprenticeship requirement for opticians was struck down in *Blumenthall* v. *Board of Medical Examiners* in 1962. The result of apprenticeship requirements has been that a person can be blocked from a profession unless a licensed professional wishes for him or her to enter the profession (Howard, 1978; Rose, 1979).

Experience requirements are sometimes imposed. In the Supreme Court decision in *Whitcomb* v. *Emerson,* the due process clause was applied to the constitutionality of an experience requirement for a face masseuse. Ruling that the experience and examination were unrelated to the occupation in question, the Court stated that the result of the statute was taking property without due process of law (Howard, 1978). Experience requirements can also have the effect of allowing existing competitors to have great control over applicants (Rose, 1979).

Examinations

Before discussing the validity issues of examinations, a distinction will be made between certification, employment testing, performance testing, and licensing.

Certification is a voluntary program that enables individuals to improve their marketability by granting them a special status (Johnson and Corgel, 1983; Hecht, 1979). Lack of certification does not usually exclude persons from practice, as is the case with licensing (Johnson and Corgel, 1983). Since the question of validity considers the purpose for which the test is used, it is important to distinguish between licensure and certification. Often, however, the terms are used interchangeably. Hecht (1979) points out that teaching certification is a misnomer, since it is a legal requirement to begin teaching and indicates no special status within the profession.

Employment testing is designed to identify applicants who potentially will be the most successful in a particular position. The nature of instruments used in licensing and employment testing differs according to the type of competency that must be demonstrated (Science Management Corporation, 1982). Obtaining a certain score on a licensing exam justifies awarding a license; obtaining a certain score on an employment test justifies awarding a job.

Performance testing is a type of occupational testing that merits bonuses within a job. Those who take performance tests are already in a job. Passing a performance test results in a change of rating.

Licensing is a mandatory program designed to protect the public health, safety, and welfare (Science Management Corporation, 1982). The occupational group itself requires that minimal job-related standards be met in order to prevent incompetent practitioners from entering practice (Johnson and Corgel, 1983; Hecht, 1979). The purpose of licensing tests is not to predict success on a particular job, but rather to indicate that the individual has demonstrated the minimal knowledge, skills, and abilities (KSA's) necessary within the occupation (Science Management Corporation, 1982; Kane, 1982).

The appropriate type of validity to consider in evaluating licensure examinations is content validity. Based on job analysis, content validity measures minimal standards necessary for competent practice. The possession of minimal knowledge, skills, and abilities related to a particular job should ensure the protection of the public's health, safety, and welfare (Science Management Corporation, 1982; Shimberg, 1981; Kane, 1982). Sandman and Urban (1976) use the term "rational validity" when referring to content validity of licensure examinations.

Criterion validity, also called empirical, concurrent, and predictive validity (Sandman and Urban, 1976), has been suggested by some as being the most appropriate for licensing exams. In practice, however, criterion validity is not used. First, it would be impossible to establish criterion validity without great expenditures of money on studies for each specific occupation to be licensed. Second, there are problems in conducting studies of the predictive validity of a licensure exam. Those who do not pass are not allowed to practice, so it is impossible to determine if those who pass the exam do better in practice than those who fail (Kane, 1982).

Construct validity is also used to predict success on a job. It measures psychological constructs or characteristics important for job success (Science Management Corporation, 1982; Shimberg, 1981). Construct validity contains elements of content and criterion validity. It is occupation-specific and depends upon the particular profession. (See chapters Two, Three, and Four in this book for further discussion of testing and validity.)

Even though validity issues of occupational tests have not been heard in the Supreme Court, many licensing agencies are adhering to the standards established in the Uniform Guidelines and *Principles for the Validation and Use of Personnel Selection Procedures,* written by the American Psychological Association's Division of Industrial and Organizational Psychology and discussed by Shimberg (1981).

Other Legal Issues

Grandfathering. Schoenhaus (1980) cites several cases in which architects were granted licenses when they had been practicing prior to the passage of statutes requiring licenses. In *Linder* v. *Copeland* (1958) the court held that the governing board acted arbitrarily in denying a license to a person who had been practicing architecture for fifteen years. Similarly, in *Waier* v. *State Board of Registration* (1942), the court held that an applicant with twelve years' practice as an architect be granted a license even though he had been employed as an engineer during that period.

Permanence of Licensing—Re-examination. One way of assuring continued competence of licensees is to re-examine them. Although a number of states now require professionals to complete a certain number of credits in continuing education, no state has insisted on periodic re-examination. Michigan's new public health code mandates that its licensing boards set up pilot programs to assess continued competence of its licensed professionals. In six years, the best of those methods piloted will be adopted to ensure continued professional competence. In no cases will licenses be permanent: those licensed will have to seek renewal at least every four years (Shimberg, 1981).

Reciprocity. The right of an individual to pursue a vocation is protected by due process. At the same time, by virtue of police power, each state may restrict practice of a particular occupation to those licensed within the state (Schoenhaus, 1980). Interstate mobility of practitioners in a regulated occupation can be greatly reduced by this right of restriction given to states if the receiving state does not practice reciprocity or endorsement. Reciprocity agreements are compacts between two states to honor their respective licenses. Endorsements are state agreements to honor the license of another state if the standards in that state are comparable (Shimberg, 1981). The low number of these agreements serves to limit mobility of practitioners of technical occupations or professions, though there is variation among occupations in regard to the number of states that practice either reciprocity or endorsement. The distance that a prospective employee is expected to move increases with the level of education and decreases with age (Pashigian, 1979).

Revocation. "The right of a qualified individual to practice his profession or vocation is, at the very least, a property right and is fully protected by the due process clause of the Fifth and Fourteenth amendments" (Ripstra, 1977, p. 296). This right to practice must be balanced with the state's authority to regulate occupations under its police power (Ripstra, 1977).

As an exercise of that power, the state which granted a license may also revoke or suspend it if sufficient cause is shown (Wagner, 1974). In the case of revocation or suspension, the licensee must be granted due process of law. Ripstra (1977) cites the case of *Greenfield* v. *Hamrick* (1976) wherein a license to practice medicine was revoked by the Alabama State Board of Medical Examiners because the defendant had been convicted by a federal court of distributing controlled substances. The revocation was reversed by the court because constitutional due process was not followed.

Although due process must be adhered to, it is not necessary that a judicial hearing be held in the case of revocation. The procedures established must be followed in order to protect the individual's rights, but the hearing may be held by the administrative board (Wagner, 1974).

The authority which granted the license has the inherent power to revoke it. Usually, however, the provisions for revocation are spelled out. The vagueness of regulations for revoking architects' licenses has been challenged in terms of the validity of statutes so worded. Vagueness was rejected as an argument in *Markel* v. *Florida State Board of Architecture* (1951). The court held that statutes authorizing revocation of an architect's license if he attached his name to plans that he neither executed nor directly supervised were clear enough for a person of ordinary knowledge to comprehend (Wagner, 1974). On appeal, however, *Markel* v. *Florida* was modified and revocation was deemed too severe a punishment. Instead, the license was suspended.

When administrative suspension or revocation has been carried out on the ground of "gross incompetency or recklessness in the construction of buildings" (Wagner, 1974, p. 555) by architects, it has been held by the courts that disciplinary action could be taken only if sufficient evidence of wrongdoing was presented. Thus, the court in *Braucher* v. *Board of Examiners of Architects* (1918) reversed the administrative board's decision when the only incompetence charged was the sale of plans for buildings that were not properly constructed (Wagner, 1974).

Zitter (1983) discusses cases in which real estate brokers' licenses have been revoked or suspended for unacceptable conduct even if not associated with business as brokers. One of the most recent of these is *Wright* v. *State* (1981), in which the broker's dishonesty was deemed proof of his unworthiness to practice. The court indicated that if a broker proved to be dishonest outside of his practice, it would be assumed he would be dishonest within his practice, as well.

Enforcement. In spite of the complicated requirements of various licensing statutes, there are comparatively few provisions for enforcement of those statutes. For example, in 1976 New York had seven people assigned to investigate 55,000 physicians. A 1974 study in Florida revealed that fewer than one percent of their licensees were investigated each year. In other cases, the licensing agencies seemed to have sufficient budgets to perform more investigations than were reported (Baron, 1980).

Baron identifies three weaknesses of licensing that contribute to its ineffectiveness. The first is the assumption that a license holder knows what he or she is doing. The license merely indicates that at one time the holder demonstrated minimal competency for the occupation. The second weakness is the lack of realistic means of enforcement. Minor violations cannot be credibly threatened with revocation or suspension of licenses. The third weakness is the inefficiency that would be inherent in any enforcement system. Resources would be wasted in attempting to supervise those licensed practitioners who do not need supervision.

Sunset Laws. If the authority of an agency up for legislative review is not renewed by its state legislature, the agency will "fade away into the sunset." Sunset laws, or nonrenewal of state agencies, have focused on almost all regulatory boards and commissions since the first such law was passed in Colorado in 1976.

The effect of sunset laws has been that regulatory boards are monitoring themselves more closely. In addition, coordinating boards have been established to evaluate the effectiveness of licensing boards. Outcomes of sunset laws are discussed more thoroughly by Shimberg in Chapter One.

Effect of Licensing. The intent of licensing, to protect the public health, safety, and welfare, has often been overshadowed by its effect, which is "sanctioned self-regulation" (Bradley, 1977). Licensing has been welcomed by members of licensed occupations to protect them against new competition (Gellhorn, 1976).

The result of licensing statutes is often the restriction of entrance into regulated occupations. According to Gellhorn, "it has . . . badly eroded the right to work, one of man's most precious liberties" (1976, p. 11). Baron (1980) advocates an alternative system that he attributes to Friedman. Practitioners could become certified, if they chose, and the public would be able to choose between certified and uncertified workers. Results would include reducing costs and the anticompetitive effects of licensing. In any case, a study of the reasons for licensing some occupations and not others as a means of evaluating the merits of licensing warrants further attention (Pashigian, 1979).

Legal Cases Cited

American Medical Association v. *United States* 318 U.S. 200 (1943)

Barbers Commission v. *Hardeman* 21 So. 2d 118 (1945)

Barsky v. *Board of Regents* 347 U.S. 422 (1954)

Bell v. *Georgia Dental Association* 231 F. Supp. 299 (1964)

Blumenthall v. *Board of Medical Examiners* 57 Cal. 228 (1962)

Board of Regents v. *Roth* 408 U.S. 564 (1972)

Braucher v. *Board of Examiners of Architects* 209 Ill. App. 455 (1918)

Butchers' Union v. *Crescent City Co.* 111 U.S. 746 (1884)

City of Tucson v. *Stewart* 45 Ariz. 36 (1935)

Examining Board of Engineers, Architects, and Surveyors v. *Florez de Otero* 426 U.S. 572 (1976)

Federal Baseball Club v. *National League* 259 U.S. 200 (1922)

Goldfarb v. *Virginia State Bar* 421 U.S. 773 (1975)

Gordon v. *Committee on Character and Fitness* 422 N.Y.S.2d 641 (1980)

Greenfield v. *Hamrick* 341 So. 2d 136 (1976)

Hampton v. *Mow Dun Wong* 96 S. Ct. 1895 (1976)

In re Griffiths 413 U.S. 717 (1973)

Linder v. *Copeland* 137 Colo. 53 (1958)

Lockner v. *New York* 198 U.S. 45 (1905)

Markel v. *Florida State Board of Architecture* 253 So. 2d 914 (1951)

Markel v. *Florida State Board of Architecture* 268 So. 2d 374 (1972)

Meyer v. *Nebraska* 262 U.S. 390 (1923)

National Society of Professional Engineers v. *United States* 433 U.S. 679 (1978)

Parrish v. *Board of Commissioners of Alabama State Bar* 524 F.2d 98 (1976)

People v. *Beattie* 89 N.Y.S. 193 (1904)

People v. *Brown* 95 N.E.2d 888 (1950)

People v. *Masters* 49 Ill. 2d 224 (1971)

Puntilillo v. *New Hampshire Racing Commission* 375 F. Supp. 1089 (1975)

Re Florida Board of Bar Examiners 358 So. 2d 7 (1978)
Richardson v. *McFadden* 540 F.2d 744 (1976)
Schware v. *Board of Bar Examiners* 353 U.S. 232 (1957)
Sheley v. *Alaska Bar Association* 620 P.2d 640 (1980)
Sibley Memorial v. *Wilson* 340 F. Supp. 686 (1973)
Spears v. *State Bar of California* 211 Cal. 183 (1931)
Standard Oil Co. v. *United States* 221 U.S. 1 (1911)
Tyler v. *Vickery* 517 F.2d 1089 (1975)
United States v. *National Association of Real Estate Boards* 339 U.S. 485 (1950)
United States v. *Oregon Medical Society* 34 U.S. 326 (1952)
Waier v. *State Board of Registration* 303 Mich. 360 (1942)
Whitcomb v. *Emerson* 115 P.2d 892 (1941)
Williamson v. *Lee Optical* 348 U.S. 483 (1955)
Wright v. *State* 208 Neb. 467 (1981)

References

Baron, D. S. "Licensing: The Myth of Government Protection." *Barrister,* 1980, *8,* 46-50.

Bradley, M. J. "The Challenge to Occupational Licensing Laws for Funeral Directors by Direct Cremation Businesses: An Examination and Proposed Solution." *Florida State University Law Review,* 1977, *5,* 381-422.

Cathcart, J. A., and Graff, G. "Occupational Licensing: Factoring It Out." *Pacific Law Journal,* 1978, *9,* 147-163.

Equal Employment Opportunity Commission and others. "Adoption by Four Agencies of Uniform Guidelines on Employment Selection Procedures." *Federal Register,* 1978, *43,* 38290-38315.

Gellhorn, W. "The Abuse of Occupational Licensing." *The University of Chicago Law Review,* 1976, *44,* 6-27.

Hall, G. L. "Annotation. Pardon as Restoring Public Office or License or Eligibility Thereof." *American Law Review 3rd,* 1974, *58,* 1091-1114.

Hecht, K. A. "Current Status and Methodological Problems of Validating Professional Licensing and Certification Exams." In M. A. Bunda and J. R. Sanders (Eds.), *Practices and Prob-*

lems in Competency-Based Education. Washington, D.C.: National Council on Measurement in Education, 1979.

Howard, G. H. "Professional Self-Regulation." *Alabama Law Review,* 1978, *29,* 679-715.

Johnson, S. B., and Corgel, J. B. "Antitrust Immunity and the Economics of Occupational Licensing." *American Business Law Journal,* 1983, *20,* 471-490.

Kane, M. T. "The Validity of Licensure Examinations." *American Psychologist,* 1982, *37,* 911-918.

Miller, E. H. "Annotation. Sexual Conduct or Orientation as Ground for Denial of Admission to Bar." *American Law Review 4th,* 1983, *21,* 1109-1113.

Pashigian, B. P. "Occupational Licensing and the Interstate Mobility of Professionals." *The Journal of Law and Economics,* 1979, pp. 1-25.

Ripstra, S. "Constitutional Law—Due Process. Hearing Required Before Revoking a Physician's License for Conviction of a Felony." *Cumberland Law Review,* 1977, *8,* 295-305.

Rose, J. "Occupational Licensing: A Framework for Analysis." *Arizona State Law Journal,* 1979, pp. 189-202.

Sandman, B., and Urban, R. "Employment Testing and the Law." *Labor Law Journal,* 1976, pp. 39-55.

Schoenhaus, R. M. "Annotation. Grant or Denial of License to Practice Architecture." *American Law Review 4th,* 1980, *2,* 1103-1109.

Science Management Corporation. "Review of the Legal Issues Related to the Design and Validation of the Licensing Examination Process." Oakridge National Laboratory Contract, unpublished report, 1982.

Shimberg, B. "Testing for Licensure and Certification." *American Psychologist,* 1981, *36,* 1138-1146.

Smith, J. K. "Production of Licensing Legislation: An Economic Analysis of Interstate Differences." *The Journal of Legal Studies,* 1982, *11,* 117-137.

Voigt, J. R. "Recent Decisions. Administrative Law—Delegation of Legislative Authority—Professional Licensure." *Emory Law Journal,* 1980, *58,* 543-555.

Wagner, F. D. "Annotation. Revocation or Suspension of Licenses to Practice Architecture." *American Law Review,* 1974, pp. 543-556.

Zitter, J. M. "Annotation. Revocation or Suspension of Real Estate Broker's License for Conduct Not Associated with Business as Broker." *American Law Review 4th,* 1983, *22,* 136-170.

6

Validation as a Formative Process: Developing Licensure Examinations for Nuclear Power Plant Operators

David J. Bowering
Jim C. Fortune
Michael T. Wood

Prior to the technology-driven proliferation of licensing and the civil rights movement, the validity of a licensing examination was almost never questioned. Needed regulation was enacted into law and the mechanics of licensing were made operational without public arousal. Any validation of the licensing examinations usually was conducted after the regulatory system had enjoyed a substantial history of operation and after several prior administrations of the examination had occurred.

Before occupational licensing became a subject of public concern, licensure testing was not differentiated from other occupational testing in regard to validation study procedures. The traditional approach to validation in occupational testing relied heavily on the establishment of criterion-related validity, and the results of the study were reported in a summative manner—either the test was accepted as valid or rejected. Since validation studies were conducted after the testing procedure was established, the role of validation study in test development was not made apparent. Hence, the finding of inadequate evidence of validity with regard to a licensing test appeared to leave the licensing agency without an alternative. In this paper we describe a case study of an approach to test validation in occupational licensing which makes the interaction between test validation and test development an important part of the licensure process.

This approach arose during our attempts to solve operational and technical problems in the development of a valid nuclear power plant reactor operator (RO) and senior reactor operator (SRO) licensing examination. The project began to materialize in 1979 when the threat to public health and safety that can result from human error in an occupation was clearly demonstrated by the "Three Mile Island" incident. Regardless of how the extent of that threat is assessed, it is undoubtedly true that human error on the part of ROs, SROs, and management resulted in a threat to human life and the environment that still lingers. This incident raised the question of whether existing licensing procedures adequately ensured the competency of plant personnel in terms of their having the necessary knowledge, skills, and abilities (KSAs) to operate that facility.

Both the Congress and the federal government reacted strongly to the Three Mile Island emergency. As a result, the Nuclear Regulatory Commission (NRC) issued a Task Action Plan that mandated improvements in the capabilities of ROs and SROs. To comply with this mandate, a programmatic study of the existing licensing examination process was undertaken and contracts were let to consulting firms with measurement and research expertise. The focus of the study was to improve this process through the use of rigorous scientific methodologies to develop a valid examination process that was demonstrably related to job performance.

The Problem

The initial work plans for the validation effort called for the conduct of a criterion validation of either the existing examination process or a 'new' examination process that might emerge from the study effort. A criterion-related validation of the existing examination process was preferred by the agency. This preference was based on the belief that a criterion-related validation would confirm or deny the ability of the licensing examination to discriminate between competent and incompetent performers on the job (in terms of the ability of ROs and SROs to operate nuclear power plants in the best interests of public health and safety).

A descriptive study of the existing examination process determined that a validation study most likely would be inconclusive because the existing process lacked the uniformity of testing procedures required in a validation study. Both the examination form and administrative procedures varied across power plants due to differences in the technical structure and equipment of the plants. The examinations, although similar in content, differed in the percentages of objective test items employed, in the use of essay and oral test strategies, and in the time required for testing. The examination process also differed across examiners who had to fit the test construction and scoring into their busy time schedules.

Analysis of the status of the RO and SRO licensing process further revealed that operator performance criteria that would satisfy both industry and government standards had not been identified. No criterion measures nor observation procedures had been developed for work requirements that might serve as performance criteria. Efforts to develop and implement such measures were deemed to be too intrusive for voluntary compliance by the industry. Furthermore, these efforts would exceed the scope of the development contracts.

Clearly, there were political, practical, and technical problems that mitigated against conducting a criterion-related validation study of the system that was in place. Diverting resources to tasks directed toward such a validation effort would have been unproductive. Instead, the development of a content validity examination and a strategy of test study was believed to be a better investment of contractor time and effort.

The Concept of Formative Validation

Formative validation is defined as a developmental, rather than definitive, process toward establishing the validity of a licensing process in which validity evidence is accumulated (1) while the examination is being developed and refined from a job analysis and (2) from analyses of data gathered in repeated administrations of the test. The term *formative validation* is meant to emphasize the nature of the test study strategy rather than to define any new type of validity evidence. It can be argued that formative content validation represents a more accurate term for the process, since most of the validity evidence accumulated addresses content-related test interpretations. Also, arguments can be made that no new terminology for the process is needed in the measurement world, since test study is frequently conducted using similar strategies. Yet, the term appears useful in client-contractor communication.

The formative process involves a study of the test development activities, the test itself, and the results of using the test—that is, interpreting the test score. The purpose is not to reject or accept the test, as is the case with post hoc validation studies, but to provide information that leads to test improvement. It is an iterative process in which information developed through successive administrations of the examination is fed back into the examination process to influence redesign, administration, and scoring. Either the content validity of the examination is documented, or threats to its validity are flagged and removed. Also gathered is longitudinal evidence of the relationship of examinee test performance to on-the-job performance regarding the association between the licensing process and safe and effective job behavior. The latter approaches a criterion-related validation process that is gradual and cumulative. There are several conceptually distinct, yet operationally related steps in the formative validation process: development of domain-referenced test content, demonstration of the content validity of the examination(s), demonstration of the quality of the item pool and revision of the item pool, and tracking the relationship between test performance on task and on-the-job task performance. These steps are not sequential, nor are they orthogonal.

Clearly, the question arises whether there is a need for further validation study, if the procedures employed to design the exams are those that meet professional standards for the development of content-valid tests. While the development procedures are such that a content-valid examination may indeed result from the development process, their use in the design process does not provide incontrovertible evidence that the resulting use of the test is content valid. The employment of professional standards in the development of a test is necessary but not of itself sufficient to ensure that content-valid interpretations can be made from the test results. Studies outside the development process are needed to demonstrate that the examinations do produce content-valid results. Each step in the process contributes evidence that allows the examination to withstand attack on any of the grounds discussed in the following sections.

Rationale for Formative Validation

In the rationale presented here for setting in place formative validation in the RO and SRO licensing examination process, it is argued that: (1) the process satisfies legal requirements emerging from court decisions regarding occupational licensing, particularly where public health and safety are involved; (2) the process permits the protection of the public from a new and immediate peril while a sound licensing system is being developed; (3) the process protects the employees' and would-be employees' civil rights by beginning with a technically sound job-analysis and state-of-the-art test development process and following through with successive test study and improvement; (4) there are methodological difficulties with existing conventional test validation strategies for occupational tests and measurements; (5) occupational conditions which confound conventional test validation strategies can be addressed or avoided by the process; and (6) formative validation permits a wide range of validation evidence to be developed over time.*

Legal Requirements. Moody v. *Albemarle Paper Co.* (474 F.2d 1324 (4th Cir., 1973)) and *Albemarle* v. *Moody* (45 L. Ed. 2d 280, 95 S. Ct. 2362 (1975)) perhaps represent the keystone cases for the establishment of judicial precedents for test validity. In *Moody* v. *Albemarle* (1973), the circuit court maintained that the occupational tests must be "job-related, and have a manifest relationship to employment." The court ruled that in the development of job performance criteria, Albemarle failed to engage in any job analysis. Instead, the test results were related to subjective supervisory ratings, thus failing to provide evidence of the validity of the tests in measuring job potential. Although this case involved an employment test instead of a licensing test, the case resulted in establishing job analysis as a second method for determining job-relatedness in legal circles. Criterion-related validity or correlational linkage between test results and job performance had been established as a legally acceptable method to establish job-relatedness in previous court cases (Sandman and Urban, 1976).

The types of evidence required by the validation process depend on the use to be made of the test. There are several types of occupational testing and several uses of test results in occupational decisions. The differences between two types, licensing and employment testing, are of relevance here.

The licensing process permits an individual to practice a profession or to engage in work requiring technical expertise only after evidence has been established that he or she is qualified. The qualifications are expressed in terms of minimum standards of knowledge, skills, and abilities required for the safe practice of the occupation. Testing in licensing is used to determine the presence of these qualifications. Although many licensing examinations or tests are scored on an interval scale, the decision concerning licensure is based upon whether or not

*This is similar to triangulation or the evidentiary process in legal proceedings. No one piece of evidence is in itself sufficient, but collectively the evidence is overwhelming and converges to one conclusion.

a candidate scores above the criterion score that has been set to reflect the required minimum standards. Hence, the decision is a dichotomous one, based on whether or not the criterion score is met.

Conversely, the purpose of employment testing is to estimate the relative potential of the candidate in regard to job performance. In this use of testing, the decision may be based on both the magnitude of the candidate's score and on whether or not the criterion score is met. Hence, validity requirements for licensing tests can be argued to be different from validity requirements for employment tests in that licensing tests are used for criterion-referenced decisions, whereas employment tests are used for norm-referenced decisions. A generally accepted evidence for the validity of tests used for criterion-referenced decisions is that of content validity (Millman, 1974). However, convincing arguments can be made for the utility of construct and criterion-related validity in criterion-referenced testing (see Chapter Three). The intended use of the test dictates the type of validity evidence required. The acceptance of content validity as evidence of test validity in occupational decisions is substantiated by several court rulings: *Riveria, Placido* v. *The City of Wichita Falls* (665 F.2d 531, 80-1332 (1982)); *United States* v. *South Carolina* (445 F. Supp. 1094 (1977)); *Vulcan Society of the City Fire Department, Inc.* v. *Civil Service Commission of the City of New York* (490 F.2d 387 (2nd Cir. 1973)).

The formative validity strategy provides for the satisfaction of validity requirements in licensing testing by: (1) establishing job-relatedness through the use of job analysis to specify the KSAs to be tested, (2) using sound measurement principles in test development to create the foundation for content validity, (3) producing evidence to substantiate content validity through the study of test performance, and (4) providing a structure through which other validity evidence can be accumulated over time.

Role of Public Peril. Methods of test validation based on the establishment of criterion-related validity require longitudinal study of test performance and evaluation of examinees' on-the-job performance. In occupations which can threaten immediate and serious public peril, regulation must begin immediately at the onset of the occupation to reduce any potential of public harm. Since regulation must occur immediately, testing for such occupations must begin with a well-developed test and then be supported by a test-study program which develops interim evidence of test validity while a long-range plan for the confirmation of validity is being implemented.

Civil Rights Concerns. Regulatory systems that are made operative without adequate study of testing are vulnerable to civil rights challenges. This vulnerability becomes greater if established training programs do not exist for the occupation in question and if the nature of the regulation is highly selective. In order to prevent civil rights challenges, the licensing system should begin with testing that has the greatest potential of being valid and racially unbiased. Tests developed from a well-planned table of specifications and based on content selected through job analysis study have the most potential for being found valid. Tests composed of items that have been screened for racial bias by a racially representative panel have the most potential for being found unbiased.

Methodological Difficulties. On-the-job performance measurement and the nature of the examinee population are sources for methodological difficulties in validation studies of licensing tests. Several difficulties exist in the choice of appropriate on-the-job measures. Too often, these measures are for only selected aspects of the job, leaving some critical parts of the job unmeasured. Efforts must be made in the test study to establish conceptual correspondence between the part measures of the job and the behaviors sampled on the test such that meaningful interpretation of the results can be made. Solitary supervisory provisions and limited opportunities for observation create difficulty in the design of reliability studies of performance measures.

Even given acceptable performance measures, the population available for the validation study may be inappropriate. Since the regulation process eliminates from the occupation examinees who score below the cut score, the population available for the validation study is truncated, producing a restricted range of scores for study. Frequently, the number of examinees available for study provide a sample that is too small for the correlational methods required in some validation efforts. Adequate time samples of worker performance are often expensive to obtain, and their collection may interfere with actual job performance. The formative validation strategy allows validation study of the test to be done incrementally such that observation of work performance can be built into the daily work schedule.

The collection of on-the-job performance data may be confounded by occupational conditions such as infrequent occurrence of some key skills or actions, work stations that do not permit direct observation or measurement, work that requires team efforts that obscure individual performance, employment of only a small number of individuals in a given position or type of work, and specialization of work where any one individual is responsible for only a small part of the total job description. Work performances in which there are no commonly agreed-upon correct reactions (such as emergency situations) but which are key job requirements can confound test scoring. The formative validation strategy has been devised to eliminate the tendency to think about test validation as a single, definitive study. Since test validation is portrayed as a longitudinal process that is conducted in several systematic efforts, time is permitted to allow experimentation with items and study of subparts of the test or of the job.

Formative Validation—The Process in Application

Context of the Application. Regulation of entry into selected occupations emerging from modern technology has become a complex and visible endeavor. The licensing agency charged with the responsibility for this regulation frequently is faced with an application of technology that requires advanced skills and several years of technical education, an occupation in which human error can produce an immediate and grave threat to public safety, government concern due to the nature of the occupation, changes in the occupation due to new technology, public scrutiny, and limited resources. The operation of nuclear power plant reactors is an excellent example of one of these emerging technical occupations for which regulation poses a problem.

Until public threat was made visible through a single incidence of human error, examination for licensing of reactor operators was conducted by a group of examiners chosen for their expertise in the highly technical occupation. Each examination administered for licensing was unique and its composition and form were both power plant- and examiner-specific. However, the licensing agency, NRC, is now faced with the problem of being able to attest to the validity of the examination process and to the competence of those licensed through it. Due to the inability to establish evidences of the validity of the idiosyncratic examinations previously in use, NRC is faced with the dilemma that regulation and licensure must continue to occur at the same time that a standardized licensing examination is being developed and validated.

We have previously described how the formative validation strategy emerged through client-contractor interaction, and we have presented the rationale used to recommend the strategy to NRC. In the remainder of this chapter we will describe the process stages that we believe belong in the application of the formative validation approach. For each stage we will delineate relevant options in methodology. Since the formative validation is now in the process of being implemented by NRC, we will report what NRC has done in those stages that have been addressed. The stages include: (1) development of domain-referenced test content, (2) development of the item pool so as to establish the foundation for content validity, (3) demonstration of the quality of the item pool, (4) conduct and use of item analysis, (5) establishment of reliability, and (6) tracking the relationship between test performance and on-the-job performance.

Development of Domain-Referenced Test Content. The first step in formative validation is the determination and specification of test content. The derivation of test content from a well-designed job analysis establishes job relatedness, a necessary condition for validity. (Note that job-relatedness does not guarantee a predictive relationship between test performance and job performance.) If means other than job analysis are used to derive content, a special study is needed to establish job-relatedness. A comprehensive and detailed job analysis was performed by the Institute for Nuclear Power Operations (INPO), and NRC was able to use the results in developing the domain-referenced content structure of the examinations.

The job analysis NRC used accounts for differences in reactor operator responsibilities due to the uniqueness in construction of the different power plants. Power plants differ in the number and type of operating systems. In the INPO job task analysis two types of plants were identified, PWR (pressurized water reactor) and BWR (boiling water reactor) plants. In the PWR plants fifty-four operating systems were documented, and in the BWR plants, thirty-one. Across all eighty-five systems, approximately seven hundred operator tasks were identified. Table 1 shows a sample of the operator tasks identified for one operating system, the main and reheat steam system.

Table 1. Sample Output of the Job Task Analysis Performed on the Operation of a Nuclear Power Plant Reactor (System 39 refers to the main and reheat steam system).

System	*Task Number*	*Task Title*
39	1	Perform a lineup of the main and reheat steam system
39	2	Perform main steam line isolation Valves full stroke test
39	3	Warmup and pressurize main steam leads
39	4	Perform main steam line isolation Valves partial stroke test
39	5	Perform a moisture separator/reheater cold start
39	6	Perform a moister separator/reheater hot start
39	7	Perform main steam line isolation Valves Trip Test
39	8	Perform hydrostatic test of reheaters
39	9	Monitor reheater operation
39	10	Dump steam through the atmospheric relief/dump valves
39	11	Shut down the main and reheat steam system

The level of abstraction in which the content is stated determines how much work must be done in organizing the content into a specification table for test development. Content should be organized and specified so as to delineate clearly the domain(s) of content to be measured. This delineation should be made in terms of discrete, nontrivial worker behaviors, if possible. The tasks delineated by the job task analyses may include several such behaviors or actions within a single task. Traditional methods of content specification use a matrix form as a means of displaying the domain structure in hierarchical levels (from the behavioral element through the task up to the system level in this case). Arraying the content in this way is not an act of documentation only. It is essential for grouping categories of similar behavior, for eliminating redundancies, for establishing the representativeness (coverage) of test items, and for guiding the actual selection and development of test items.

The tasks specified in the INPO job task analysis were not at the level of abstraction required for measurement. More than one operator action or behavior was required to complete most of the tasks. Table 2 displays a breakdown of the sample tasks shown in Table 1. Note that the behaviors derived from each task are not commonplace or trivial behaviors such as turning dials or climbing ladders. Over 1,500 behaviors were obtained from the job analysis.

Table 2. Operator Behaviors Required to Complete the Tasks Shown in the Sample Output Figure

Task Title	*Required Operator Behaviors*
Perform a Lineup of the Main and Reheat Steam System	1. Cycle the remote-operated main steam valves supplying auxiliary steam, main feedwater pump turbines, emergency feedwater pump turbines, and the moisture-separator reheaters to verify operability. 2. Perform a remotely operated valve alignment on the main and reheat steam system.
Perform Main Steam Line Isolation Valves (MSIV) Full Stroke Test	1. Verify with performance technician that computer is ready for MSIV stroke timing and that the actual test is ready to commence. 2. Verify MSIV stroking time by timing with a stopwatch.

Table 2. Operator Behaviors Required to Complete the Tasks Shown in the Sample Output Figure, Cont'd.

Task Title	*Required Operator Behaviors*
Warmup and Pressurize Main Steam Leads	1. Check S/G pressure at specified pressure to warm up steam leads. 2. Equalize main steam header and S/G pressure to within specified limits.
Perform MSIV Partial Stroke Test	1. Perform MSIV partial stroke test.
Perform a Moisture Separator/Reheater (MSR) Cold Start	1. Perform the control room portion of the moisture separator/reheater cold start lineup. 2. Perform the control room portion of the MSR piston-operated valve lineup. 3. Verify the MSR level control valves maintain proper level in the second-stage drain tanks.
Perform a Moisture Separator/Reheater Hot Start (MSRH)	1. Verify proper operation of MSRH by checking MSRH temperatures and steam pressures.
Perform Main Steam Line Isolation Valves Trip Test	1. Measure closing time of MSIV from when MSIV trip dump valve is placed in trip position to when MSIV open light extinguishes.
Perform Hydrostatic Test of Reheaters	1. Review tag out procedures for completeness and accuracy.
Monitor Reheater Operation	1. Verify main turbine exhaust pressure within operating limits. 2. Verify moisture separator/reheater temperatures within operating limits. 3. Verify MSRH steam pressure within operating limits.
Dump Steam Through the Atmospheric Relief/Dump Valves	1. Verify condenser not available for dumping steam. 2. Check tave to ensure reduction in tave is necessary.
Shut Down the Main and Reheat Steam System	1. Verify all moisture separator reheater dumps to the condenser are open.

In order to facilitate the grouping of similar behaviors and the elimination of redundancies, a classification scheme was formulated. Six types of tasks were identified across operating systems: emergency tasks, abnormal alarm conditions, normal plant operating procedures, startup/shutdown tasks, testing and surveillance tasks, and mode-change tasks. The tasks and their corresponding operator behaviors were classified and then checked for redundancies. The list of more than 1,500 operator behaviors was reduced to 700 discrete and unique operator behaviors that serve as the specified content to be examined.

The next step is to use this matrix to decide what each item is to measure. Whether by design or not, test items will necessarily measure factual knowledge in some instances, in others the ability of the examinee to synthesize facts and information to draw conclusions, and in others the ability to analyze data to identify key information and prescribe actions. These behaviors are at different levels of complexity and should not be weighted equally in importance either in designing the test or in evaluating the results.

Content should now be classified by the levels at which each behavior should be measured. These levels may include dimensions such as knowledge, comprehension, application, analysis, synthesis, and evaluation. The matrix type of content specification will enable the use of domain sampling to ensure content validity and will facilitate item development. In this case each cell is thought of as a trait for which there can be associated a domain of items which measure the trait. The amount or relative importance of content can be estimated for each cell from the task analysis. This estimation should identify the percentage of contribution that each cell is to make to the composition of the total test. Once the content proportions for the test are determined, the length of the test estimated and the type of items selected, the number of items from each cell can be determined.

Although the behaviors in the reactor operation content matrix range from reading gauges to using physical science principles to translate gauge readings into action, it was decided that each behavior could be broken down into cognitive knowledge components and enabling skill components. This breakdown of the behaviors was deemed more useful than a taxonomic breakdown due to its correspondence to plant manuals and to occupational practice. Table 3 displays the breakdown into cognitive knowledges and enabling skills for two of the tasks shown in Figure 2. These cognitive knowledges and enabling skills when referenced to the respective behaviors present adequate descriptive detail for the determination of relative importance and for the development of test items. The breakdown of the 700 behaviors resulted in approximately 5,000 cognitive knowledge and enabling skills. To this point, the job-content domain for developing test items is defined as being sets of organized KSAs that pertain to performing types of tasks essential to operating systems important to plant safety.

An additional classification of content is being considered. In this classification, the cognitive knowledges would be classified into four categories: reasoning and problem solving, procedural, applications of principles or concepts, and equipment operation or functioning. The enabling skills would be classified into the categories of manual, communication, supervisory, and team skills. This classification will be added if it is judged to aid the item development process.

Development of the Item Pool. Development of the content domain matrix is, of course, a prerequisite for developing the item pool from which the exams will be constructed. Development of a content-valid item pool is not simply a matter of writing items and matching them to the content domain matrix. The amount of time available for testing, the required turnaround time for test scoring, and the number of times that the test is to be administered influence the composition of the test.

In the NRC operator licensing exam development, the content specification has been completed to a point that some information is available about the testing system, although items are not yet developed. The item-writing effort will be directed toward the development of an item pool since item banking is planned for the composition of individual tests that will be administered on demand. The decision concerning the number of items desired for each cognitive knowledge or enabling skill has not been made since further content classification is being considered. A second decision, key to the definition of the testing system, is also under study. This decision has to do with the degree to which objective test items can be developed to measure the content. Examiners who are content experts favor the utilization of essay items and oral testing so as to indi-

Table 3. Cognitive Knowledge and Enabling Skills for the Behaviors Needed to Complete Two Illustrative Tasks.

Tasks	*Behaviors*	*Cognitive Knowledge*	*Enabling Skills*
1. Perform Main Steam Line Isolation Valves (MSIV) full stroke test	1. Verify with performance technician that computer is ready for MSIV stroke timing and that actual test is ready to commence	1. Familiarity with MSIV movement at: (a) Ability to understand and apply.	1. Ability to receive verbal reports.
		2. MSIV stroke timing ensures MSIV will not be cycled more than necessary to ensure proper operation during normal operations.	
	2. Verify MSIV stroking time by timing with a stopwatch.	1. Familiarity with MSIV movement at: (a) ability to understand and apply.	1. Skill to use stopwatch to determine operating time of motor operated valves. 2. Location of MSIV value indications. 3. Interpretation of MSIV indications.

2. Warmup and pressurize main steam leads	1. Check S/G pressure at specified pressure to warm up steam leads.	1. Specified S/G pressure required before warming main steam leads. 2. Reason for checking steam generator pressure prior to commencing warmup of steam header: (a) to ensure reactor coolant system at point of adding heat; (b) pressure temperature relationship in a saturated system. 3. Operation of plant computer to call up S/G parameters. 4. Familiarity with plant startup sop: (a) ability to understand and apply.	1. Location of steam generator pressure indication. 2. Interpretation of steam pressure indicators: (a) linear scale-reads in PSIG; (b) 3 indicators for each steam generator. 3. Location of process computer operator console.

vidualize the test to the power plant for which the examination is being administered. We believe that much of the content can be tested by objective items. Results of the item development effort will provide information in regard to the feasibility of objective items.

After the content specification has been completed, reviewed, and cleaned of redundancies, it is estimated that the content will include approximately forty-eight operating systems and will average one hundred KSAs per system. The amount of content to be tested is impressive. This content may be further reduced by aggregating skills stated with unnecessary specification into more collective skill statements. There appears to be a fair amount of latitude in the establishment of time available for testing with a work week providing an upper bound. Similar time restrictions exist for turnaround time in scoring. The number of times the test will be administered will depend on demand as defined by the requirements of the different power plants and by the availability of licensure candidates and examiners.

Knowledge in the content area being measured is not the only qualification for the developers of test items. Effective test items are usually developed through a sequence of item tryouts, reviews, and revisions. Items for the RO and SRO licensing test should be developed through collaboration between measurement specialists and subject-matter specialists.

Demonstration of the Quality of the Item Pool. The opportunity to try out test items is an important consideration in the development of a formative validation process. Prediction of how test items will perform without tryout information is virtually impossible. Items used in a test without prior study may be counterproductive to the measurement process. If the opportunity for item pretesting or tryout is not possible, there should be a provision for the adjustment of test scoring based upon item performance.

At this point in the implementation process, provision for pretesting the items developed for the RO and SRO examination appears logistically impossible. The NRC will likely opt for the development of provisions to adjust the scoring of the tests in the early administrations for unsatisfactory items.

Item reviews can provide useful information in item development. A review of the items by a panel of incumbents in the occupation and subject-matter experts to see if the items tap meaningful content should result in the elimination of trivial items. Review of each item by a panel of recent examinees for clarity, appropriateness of terminology, and instructional relevance should improve the quality of the items. The third form of review is directed toward the elimination of cultural and racial bias. In this review a panel composed of subgroup members reviews the items in the pool so as to eliminate potential discriminatory wording. Methods exist to study content validity quantitatively. These methods involve the use of item content ratings matched to either objectives or KSAs by content specialists (Rovinelli and Hambleton, 1977).

Several study techniques offer the potential for test improvement after a sufficient number of administrations of the tests have accrued to provide adequate sample sizes and to have sufficient replications to assess the stability of item performance. These techniques can provide rules for item selection in terms of difficulty and discrimination indices, measure item bias, and estimate the dimensionality of a form of the test. Most, but not all, of these test study techniques involve some form of item analysis.

Several factors influence the choice among the alternatives for test study that are available in the formative process. These factors include:

- The RO and SRO examinations are criterion-referenced rather than norm-referenced tests.
- A criterion-referenced use of the test information may require a different form of reliability, different evidences of validity, and different interpretations of item discrimination and difficulty indices from a norm-referenced use of the test information.
- The test administration requirements influence the

availability of data, the availability of time to analyze the data, the use of test study information, and the type of test used.

- The type of test employed influences the type of item statistics possible, the options available for item revision and replacement, and the test scoring system.
- The population of examinees will determine the nature of test study designs and the interpretation of item statistics.

Content and Use of Item Analysis. Difficulty and discrimination analyses are two standard techniques in item analysis. Both indices can be used in the generation of item selection rules, identifying items which are not performing as intended, and some item bias studies.

In determining item difficulty, several methods are used by measurement specialists to analyze difficulty levels of specific items. The simplest measure of item difficulty is the proportion method (Anastasi, 1976; Hecht and Swineford, 1981), which defines difficulty in terms of the percentage of people answering an item correctly. This method provides only minimal information in criterion-referenced testing.

In addition to the proportion method, many specialists compute a difficulty index "delta" for each item according to the proportion correct (Anastasi, 1976; Hecht and Swineford, 1981). This method provides useful information, but it is dependent on the assumption of a normal distribution of scores. A criterion-referenced licensing examination which is designed to test mastery cannot be expected to meet this assumption.

An alternative to "delta" that we recommend is the "Phi coefficient" (Wild, 1975). It is based on four different conditions: masters answering an item correctly, masters answering an item incorrectly, nonmasters answering an item correctly; and nonmasters answering an item incorrectly. The coefficient gives those designing the examination a "signal" that suggests re-evaluation of particular items. In mastery testing, items are usually expected to have coefficients greater than .80.

A discrimination index shows the extent to which an item is able to differentiate between examinees performing well on the test and those performing poorly. Biserial correlations are generally used with criterion-referenced tests in the determination of item discrimination. The reason for the frequent use of this type of correlation is the fact that the biserial coefficient is an indication of the relationship between the examinees who answer an item correctly with those who answer incorrectly on the basis of a criterion score (Walker, 1981; Plumbe, 1980). The point biserial correlation is used with criterion-referenced tests that are used to determine mastery. Point biserial correlation is a more easily interpreted and computed variation of the biserial correlation (Plumbe, 1980; Wild, 1975). The authors recommend this as an appropriate indicator.

The authors have recommended that both the Phi and point biserial coefficients be included in the item bank as aids in item selection for test construction. We recommend the use of analyses of item performance and analyses of choice of item distractors across subgroups (age, sex, race, training background, and examiners) to better understand the testing performance.

A final set of test study methods involves the study of standard-setting techniques. Methods for setting standards include judgmental methods based on item content (Ebel, 1962), on the probability of correct answers by minimally competent examinees developed by Angoff (Brennan and Lockwood, 1980), on guessing (Millman, 1974), on empirical methods including the data criterion measure (Livingston, 1975) and the decision-theoretic approach (Kriewell, 1972), and on combination methods including contrasting groups (Zieky and Livingston, 1977), borderline groups (Berk, 1976), and Bayesian methods (Hambleton and Novick, 1973).

Shikiar (1983) in a paper prepared for NRC reviewed cut-score requirements in the light of the licensing mandate and the examination development effort. He recommended that NRC consider the application of multiple methods for deriving cut scores. The Angoff and the contrasting groups methods appear to be promising methods. Other recommendations were that the current implicit judgmental process used by the examiners should be made explicit so as to result in increased technical justification of the cut scores, and that NRC recognize that the establishment of cut scores for the operating portions of the examination is fraught with problems and will represent new exploration of the methodology.

Establishment of Reliability. Reliability is related to the validity of a test in that reliability can be defined as a measure of the extent to which there is random error in the test scores. If the reliability of a test is too low, then the validity can be lost in false interpretations caused by the influence of these errors.

In criterion-referenced testing there are generally three major conceptualizations of reliability. They are a decision consistency approach involving the consistency of mastery-nonmastery decision making across repeated measures with one test form or parallel test forms, an approach involving the consistency of individual scores about the cut score, and an approach involving the consistency of individual scores across parallel or randomly parallel test forms.

Perhaps the approach to reliability most germane to the licensure decision is the consistency of decisions analogue. Several models exist for the estimation of this form of criterion-referenced reliability. Among these models are those of Carver (1970) and of Swaminathan, Hambleton, and Algina (1974), which require the administration of the same test twice or the administration of parallel forms of the same test, and those of Huynh (1976), Subkoviak (1976) and Marshall and Haertel (1976), which require only a single administration of the test.

Models to estimate squared deviations from cut scores include the early model of Livingston (1975) and the generalizability theory model of Brennan and Kane (1977). This estimate of reliability is referred to as an index of dependability. In generalizability theory it is referenced as an index of agreement. Chapter Four of this volume provides a more detailed treatment of reliability considerations. A full treatment of computation procedures is included in Berk (1980).

The RO and SRO examinations, regardless of this development effort, will still have some sources of inconsistency, such as variability in item form, differences in administration times and settings, and differences in examiners. These inconsistencies compound the estimation of reliability. Another confounding factor in the estimation of reliability is the expected lack of variability in the criterion-referenced test (CRT) scores due to the high level of qualification required for ROs and SROs. Reliability measures traditionally rely on correlations, and when variability is low, correlation estimates tend to be low and reliability indications based on them are misleading. For example, it is possible for an examination to be perfectly consistent, yet the reliability indices may indicate a poor-quality instrument (Buck, 1975). The NRC has indicated that parallel administrations of the examination are not possible logistically or politically. Hence, models to estimate CRT reliability that require two administrations of the test are eliminated from consideration. Of the other models, two approaches appear likely for NRC adoption. The approach of Subkoviak (1976) and the generalizability analysis approach of Brennan and Kane (1977) are models which the NRC may adopt.

Tracking the Relationship Between Test Performance and On-the-Job Performance. The final step in the implementation of the formative validation strategy is the development of supplementary evidences of validity. This step approximates a criterion-related validation in that the focus is on the study of the relationship between job performance and test scores. However, construct validation studies can be designed in this step if desired. Scores on subsets of items organized by task can be archived by examinee in order to permit longitudinal study of item relationship to job performance, and the subsequent longitudinal study will again result in item revision and refinement. With each successive administration, evaluation, study, and the subsequent revision of the item pool, the amount of validation evidence and the validity of subsequent examinations increase.

Criterion-related validity refers to the extent that a test predicts examinee performance on an external criterion that is considered to provide a direct measure of the characteristic or behavior in question. The methods through which criterion-related validity can be investigated include correlational study between the test's performance and that of another test purporting to measure the same thing (concurrent validity) and correlational study of the ability of the test to predict some external criterion posited to be a direct measure of the content of interest (predictive validity). Dunnette (1966) describes three other methods of generating preliminary evidence of criterion-related validity. They are synthetic validation, multidimensional scatter plotting validation, and experimental validation. The process of synthetic validation attempts to show that the test predicts selected behavior that has, through prior study, been shown necessary to a job. The multidimensional scatter plotting is a method proposed by Dunnette that associates test performance, worker characteristics, and several measures of job performance on a multidimensional map. The experimental validation method is similar in design to Brown's (1976) separate groups validation model. It is likely that a traditional correlation study will suffice for the NRC example studied here.

The tracking of examinees in their practice of the occupation is essential for the design of any criterion-related validation study. Even if the total test forms cannot be subjected to correlational analysis with job performance because total job performance information cannot be gained, items can be related to selected job performances and to surrogate measures, such as longevity on the job. The design of the formative validation process may require the tagging of a selected sample of examinees for whom detailed job performance data are collected, or it may be to track all examinees and use whatever job-performance information is available. Tracking may be conducted through agreements with examinees or through agreements with management in the occupation, or simply through regular record keeping.

This step in the formative validation process should include the following components in preparation for a longitudinal test study:

- A system for tracking examinees
- A record system for documenting and storing examinees' work performance and work records
- A planning and study effort to develop job performance criteria
- A record system to accumulate examinee test performance records

The ultimate product of this aspect of the process should be several attempts at the establishment of concurrent or criterion-related validity using both the Dunnette models and the traditional model.

The NRC has committed to the creation of the record-keeping system and the development of the system for tracking examinees. It is anticipated that the record-keeping and tracking systems will be completed as part of the current examination development effort.

Overall, the formative validation process should provide the support system necessary for the emergence over time of a legal and effective regulatory testing system. It can be set in place gradually, and it is a tool for test development that should be followed elsewhere, even though the RO and SRO test validation is something of an atypical example.

References

Anastasi, A. *Psychological Testing.* (4th ed.) New York: Macmillan, 1976.

Berk, R. A. "Determination of Optimal Cutting Scores in Criterion-Referenced Measurement." *Journal of Experimental Education,* 1976, *45,* 4-9.

Berk, R. A. (Ed.). *Criterion-Referenced Measurement: The State of the Art.* Baltimore, Md.: Johns Hopkins University Press, 1980.

Berk, R. A. (Ed.). *Handbook of Methods of Detecting Test Bias.* Baltimore, Md.: Johns Hopkins University Press, 1982.

Brennan, R. L., and Kane, M. T. "An Index of Dependability for Masters Tests." *Journal of Educational Measurement,* 1977, *14,* 277-289.

Brennan, R. L., and Lockwood, R. E. "A Comparison of the Nedelsky and Angoff Cutting Score Procedures Using Generalizability Theory." *Applied Psychological Measurement,* 1980, pp. 219-240.

Brown, F. G. *Principles of Educational and Psychological Testing.* New York: Holt, Rinehart and Winston, 1976.

Buck, L. S. *Use of Criterion-Referenced Tests in Personnel Selection: A Summary Status Report.* Washington, D.C.: Test

Services Section, Personnel Research and Development Center, U.S. Civil Service Commission, 1975.

Carver, R. P. "Special Problems in Measuring Change with Psychometric Devices." In *Evaluation Research: Strategies and Methods.* Pittsburgh, Penn.: American Institute for Research, 1970.

Cronbach, L. J. "Test Validation." In R. L. Thorndike (Ed.), *Educational Measurement.* Washington, D.C.: American Council on Education, 1976.

Dunnette, M. D. *Personnel Selection and Placement.* Belmont, Calif.: Wadsworth, 1966.

Ebel, R. L. "Content Standard Test Scores." *Educational and Psychological Measurement,* 1962, *22,* 15-25.

Hambleton, R. K., and Eignor, D. R. "Guidelines for Evaluating Criterion-Referenced Tests and Test Manuals." *Journal of Educational Measurement,* 1978, *15,* 321-377.

Hambleton, R. K., and Novick, M. R. "Toward an Integration of Theory and Method for Criterion-Referenced Tests." *Journal of Educational Measurement,* 1973, *10,* 154-170.

Hecht, L. W., and Swineford, F. *Item Analysis at Educational Testing Service.* Princeton, N.J.: Educational Testing Service, 1981.

Huynh, H. "On the Reliability of Decisions in Domain-Referenced Testing." *Journal of Educational Measurement,* 1976, *13,* 256-264.

Kriewell, T. E. "Aspects and Applications of Criterion-Referenced Tests." Paper presented to the American Educational Research Association, Chicago, Feb. 1972.

Linn, R. L. "Issues of Validity in Measurement for Competency-Based Programs." In M. A. Bunda and J. R. Sanders (Eds.), *Practices and Problems in Competency-Based Education.* Washington, D.C.: Council on Measurement in Education, 1979.

Livingston, S. A. *A Utility-Based Approach to the Evaluation of Pass/Fail Testing Decision Procedures.* Princeton, N.J.: Center for Occupational and Professional Assessment, Educational Testing Service, 1975.

Marshall, J. L., and Haertel, E. H. "The Mean Split-Half Coefficient of Agreement: A Single Administration Index Reliability for Mastery Tests." Unpublished manuscript, University of Wisconsin, 1976.

Martuza, V. O. *Applying Norm-Referenced and Criterion-Referenced Measurement in Education.* Boston: Allyn & Bacon, 1977.

Messick, S. A. "The Standard Problem: Measuring and Values in Measurement and Evaluation." *American Psychologist,* 1975, *20,* 955-966.

Millman, J. "Criterion-Referenced Measurement." In W. J. Popham (Ed.), *Evaluation in Education: Current Applications.* Berkeley, Calif.: McCutchan, 1974.

Plumbe, L. B. *A Guide to the Development of Job Knowledge and Skill Tests: A Reference Kit for Measurement Specialists.* (2nd ed.) Washington, D.C.: Education Services Branch, Personnel Research and Development Center, Office of Personnel Management, 1980.

Rovinelli, R. J., and Hambleton, R. K. "On the Use of Content Specialists in the Assessment of Criterion-Referenced Test Validity." *Dutch Journal of Educational Research,* 1977, *2,* 49-60.

Sandman, B., and Urban, R. "Employment Testing and the Law." *Labor Law Journal,* 1976, pp. 39-55.

Shikiar, R. *Establishing Cut Scores for the NRC Reactor Operator and Senior Reactor Operator Exam.* Washington, D.C.: U.S. Nuclear Regulatory Commission, 1983.

Shimberg, B., Esser, B. F., and Kruger, D. H. *Occupational Licensing Practices and Policies.* Washington, D.C.: Public Affairs Press, 1973.

Subkoviak, M. J. "Estimating Reliability from a Single Administration of a Mastery Test." *Journal of Educational Measurement,* 1976, *13,* 265-276.

Swaminathan, H.; Hambleton, R. K.; and Algina, J. "Reliability of Criterion-Referenced Tests: A Decision-Theoretic Formulation." *Journal of Educational Measurement,* 1974, *11,* 263-267.

Walker, R. C. *A Reader's Guide to Test Analysis Reports.* Princeton, N.J.: Educational Testing Service, 1981.

Wild, C. *Item Analysis, Item Selection, and Equating for Criterion-Referenced Testing.* Princeton, N.J.: Educational Testing Service, 1975.

Zieky, M. J., and Livingston, S. A. *Manual for Setting Standards on the Basic Skills Assessment Tests.* Princeton, N.J.: Educational Testing Service, 1977.

7

Developing and Implementing a State Licensing System

Theodore R. Cromack
Charles S. Coit

Hairdressers and lawyers—what do they have in common with real estate agents, doctors, plumbers, insurance agents, and electricians? The answer is that each must be licensed to practice his or her profession.

State legislatures have determined that because people acting in any one of these capacities have the power to inflict substantial harm on clients or customers, minimal standards of competence should be required. Thus the job of consumer protection, in these areas where consumers may not be able to protect themselves, has been taken on by the states. States carry out this role of policing an industry in three ways: by establishing educational requirements for the practitioner; by establishing a licensing procedure, a requirement of which may be a licensing examination; and by enforcing the laws and rules and regulations that pertain to the trade or profession in question.

The practices of the beautician, doctor, lawyer, real estate broker, and others have become complex professional services. For example, competent real estate agents must understand and be able to negotiate and, in some states, draft purchase and sale contracts; they must be able to analyze and explain a dozen mortgage types and determine which is most appropriate for a given set of circumstances. In Maine, environmental and land use laws that are unique to the state determine how and where new development can take place. These are but a few examples of the range of knowledge a competent real estate agent must have. The risks to the naive, home-buying public of working with an incompetent real estate professional are substantial. We all know of cases where families' personal savings have been wiped out as a result of inept practices by a real estate agent.

In 1937, the Maine legislature established a real estate commission to oversee the education, licensing, and regulation of the real estate brokerage business in this state. Since that time, the commission's role in policing the industry has grown. The story of how this body established one arm of its authority, its *licensure* system, may provide useful insight into a practical licensing situation.

Overview of the System

The Maine Board of Real Estate Commissioners is charged with the responsibility for defining and maintaining the level of quality of real estate practice in the state. The primary method of discharging this responsibility is to control entry into the real estate sales and broker fields by licensing salespersons and brokers.

To qualify for a license to practice real estate sales or brokering, a resident must demonstrate adequate knowledge and skills of the law and established procedural requirements by taking a written examination. Before registering to take the broker's examination, the person must have completed a course in real estate law, in real estate valuation, and in real estate practice. These courses, taught by qualified and experienced brokers, appraisers, and lawyers, were established by the board of commissioners to enhance the quality of real estate practice. Originally taught on an "as needed" basis, the courses have been grouped into a coherent curricula within the Center for Real Estate Education of the University of Southern Maine, in Portland. Candidates for the salesperson's license are not required to take the broker's courses. They must, however, pass an examination covering the same substantive material, and if successful on the examination, they are licensed to work for a broker who is responsible for their works. A salesperson may not practice on his or her own.

Exceptions to the training requirement for entry into the real estate profession are permitted for persons who hold a sales or broker license valid in another state. However, these persons must take the Maine examination. Since entry is largely controlled through the course satisfaction requirement, the system is relatively well documented and communicated. The courses are based on Maine standards of practice and have been developed after analyzing the professional tasks and responsibilities for salespersons and brokers within the state of Maine.

History of the Present Licensure Examination

Real estate brokerage in the United States is governed by laws and practices that are as varied as the fifty jurisdictions that make the federal union. Each state has its own real estate board, its own licensing laws, and its own rules and regulations reflecting the practices of that jurisdiction. Brokerage practices vary significantly from state to state. For example: "In Maine, real estate brokers routinely complete purchase and sale contracts for residential real estate transfers. Contrast this brokerage function with the practice in Massachusetts, where purchase and sale contracts are drafted by attorneys. The skills required of a broker in Maine and Massachusetts are clearly different. That which is satisfactory practice in Massachusetts is not satisfactory in Maine" (Coit, 1979, p. 21).

In addition to varying laws, rules and regulations, and practices, each jurisdiction has different educational requirements for licensure. According to the 1979 annual report of the National Association of Real Estate License Law Officials (NARELLO), requirements range from no formal educational prerequisite in Alaska, the District of Columbia, Indiana, Missouri, New Hampshire, West Virginia, and Wyoming to the more stringent standards of California, Texas, and Pennsylvania, which require college-level courses and experience as a salesperson. (California requires two years' full-time sales experience, plus six three-unit college-level courses.)

The basic question, therefore, is: Will a test that is satisfactory for Massachusetts or California adequately serve the people of Maine? Will a test for licensure in a state where there is no educational prerequisite be appropriate for a jurisdiction where college course credit is required?

State-Specific Courses. The Maine Board of Real Estate Commissioners has approached its educational and licensing responsibilities in a methodical fashion. First, the commission developed the three prelicensing courses to prepare licensure applicants for the brokerage profession. The content of each course is precisely delineated in extensive course syllabi written for the commission by Maine practitioners. The key ingredient to these three courses is their unique relevance to Maine. The real estate law course was designed by Maine attorneys to address state statutes that brokers must know to practice competently in Maine. For example, two recent Maine court cases, *Bourgoin* v. *Fortier* (Me. 310 A.2d 618 (1977)) and *Chapman* v. *Bomann* (Me. 381 A.2d 1123 (1978)) affect two critical areas of brokerage practice—listing contracts and purchase and sales contracts. These cases are law in Maine, and although their holdings are highly persuasive, it is uncertain, indeed doubtful, that they are recognized as law in other jurisdictions where the specific issues have not been tested.

Similarly, the property valuation course was designed with the same philosophy—a course for Maine brokers that deals in issues of valuation of Maine properties. Maine is a predominantly rural state with a substantial tourist immigration during the summer months and seasonal populations in the coastal and lake regions; businesses are characteristically small, often "mom and pop" shops. The property valuation course reflects these realities.

The real estate practice course, designed to teach brokers the essentials of competent practice, is built around the extensive and detailed requirements of Maine license law. The law, rules, and regulations have been developed over years of Maine experience and are designed both to protect the public and to guide the broker in his business. Maine's license law imposes special obligations on the broker not imposed on brokers in other parts of the country.

Examination Development. A proposal was presented to the board of commissioners by the Center for Real Estate Education after lengthy discussion with consultants. The proposal, tempered with known realities of the Maine economic situation, covered a procedure for developing, administering, maintaining, scoring, and reporting the results of an examination for licensing salespersons and brokers in Maine.

Content Validity. As with all tests, the validity of the test depends upon the validity of the items. The test items were developed from the course material and curriculum used in the courses previously described. The validity of the content of the courses was established as follows. The real estate commission conducted a task analysis of the job of a real estate broker by mailing a questionnaire to a selected number of licensed Maine brokers. The results of this survey yielded a large number of tasks that the commission reviewed and ranked in order of relative importance for entry-level skills. These data were given to a panel of knowledgeable persons, who drew up the curriculum content for the appropriate domains.

The University of Southern Maine's Center for Real Estate Education, whose staff had been conducting the real estate courses under contract with the commission, contracted to develop and administer the two examinations, one for salespersons and one for brokers. A workshop was established, and fourteen persons were selected on the basis of their knowledge, reputation in their respective fields (law, appraisal, and practice) and their interest in the licensure process. These experts participated as item authors and panel reviewers. Each topical area (law, valuation, and practice) had one item author and three panel reviewers with professional expertise in the area.

The workshop, designed and led by a test-development specialist, addressed several points: multiple-choice testing theory, the flexibility of multiple-choice items, and the elements of test-worthy items. Using the skills learned in the workshop, the authors and panel reviewers developed a pool of multiple-choice items that underwent several stages of scrutiny prior to their ultimate use on an examination. Because the test items were drawn from course material and curriculum guides derived from job/task analyses, the argument is made that the examination itself is content valid.

Item Analysis. Before use on an exam, items prepared by the team were administered to a group of already licensed brokers and salespersons. After such trial administration and subsequent administration of the test, item analysis data were prepared and reviewed. Items with negative discrimination factors were eliminated from scoring, and the remaining items were reviewed for difficulty and discrimination indices and refined as appropriate. For example, nonfunctional distractors were rewritten prior to item reuse on a later exam.

Review of Reliability. After each administration, reliability of the examination is examined and a thorough review is made of the potential for misinterpreting the examination results. Two administrations of the examination were reported on at a national conference in testing, and the specific characteristics of the examination are available in that paper (see Cromack, 1979, for more details).

Administration. To assure uniformity of administration at each of three test sites, a test administrator's manual was written. The manual contains directions that are read to the examinees at each site. Close attention to item security is critical and is observed at all stages of exam development, item storage, exam printing, and administration. Security is enforced by limiting access to only those who are involved in the administration process. Examination administrators at each of the locations maintain a careful receipt control system and have been impressed with the importance of following the procedures to the letter.

Description of the Examination

A full description of the tests is available in two papers (Cromack, 1979; Coit, 1979) presented in San Francisco at the annual meeting of the National Council on Measurement in Education. Only the briefest description can be provided here.

There are two examinations, one for applicants for a license as a real estate salesperson and one for applicants for a broker's license. Both examinations are given in three parts: real estate law, real estate valuation, and real estate practice. The sales examination consists of fifty items in each of the three topical areas. The passing score was established by the real estate commission at 70 percent in each of the separate areas. The broker examination consists of sixty items in each of the three topical areas, and at least 75 percent of the items in each part must be answered correctly to qualify for a broker's license.

Reliability. Reliability is normally expressed in terms of one or more of the following statistics: standard error of measurement, Kuder-Richardson split-half coefficient (KR-20), or test-retest coefficient of stability. Over the several administrations of the test, the average KR-20 coefficient has been calculated, as well as the average standard error of measurement. These two statistics are given in Table 1 for each component of the tests.

Table 1. Average Reliability Coefficients and Standard Errors of Measurement for Maine Real Estate Salesperson and Broker Licensure Examinations.

	Reliability Type	*Examination Sections*			*Examination Overall*
		Law	*Valuation*	*Practice*	
Sales	KR-20	0.800	0.747	0.733	0.761
(*N*=264)	SEMeas	3.525	3.777	3.007	n/a
Brokers	KR-20	0.653	0.727	0.688	0.690
(*N*=126)	SEMeas	3.001	3.167	2.920	n/a

Note: KR-20 = Kuder-Richardson split-half coefficient; SEMeas = standard error of measurement; n/a = not available.

Difficulty. The difficulty level of the exam has varied only slightly over the several testing cycles. The average item difficulty is the examination difficulty level. Table 2 reports the difficulty level of the overall exam and percentage of items with-

Table 2. Difficulty Level of Maine Real Estate Salesperson and Broker Licensure Examinations.

	CYCLE 12777		*CYCLE 2778*	
	Sales People Passing	*Brokers Passing*	*Sales People Passing*	*Brokers Passing*
Exam Difficulty	0.725	0.754	0.702	0.742
Percentage of Items Within Difficulty Ranges				
0.90-1.00 (Easy)	18.0	29.4	16.0	26.7
0.60-0.89 (Moderately Easy)	58.0	50.6	58.0	48.3
0.40-0.59 (Average)	19.3	15.0	19.3	17.2
0.39-below (Difficult)	4.7	5.0	6.7	7.8

in specified difficulty ranges in terms of the percentage of those passing the items.

The number of persons passing the examination when an externally fixed cut-off score is established is a further measure of the difficulty of the examination. The Maine real estate commission established the cut scores at 75 percent for brokers and 70 percent for salespersons. These are not unusual cut-off scores. Comparison with other national examinations yields relative validity and difficulty measures shown in Table 3.

Table 3. Comparative Difficulty Levels for Maine Real Estate Salesperson and Broker Examinations and Other Examinations.

Examinations Taken	*Brokers Passing*	*Sales People Passing*
Maine Center for Real Estate Education Exam	55%	46%
ETS Exam (23 states)	49%	47%
Other (national)	54%	61%

Problems and Successes. Three problems have been identified that limit the efficacy of the state-developed examination:

- Further validation studies (concurrent and predictive) have been postponed due to lack of funds.
- Funding for full computerization—item banking and item selection—is lacking.
- Mechanical problems with the grading scanner have caused irregularities in exam scoring, requiring careful manual review of scoring.

None of these problems is insolvable, and all could be resolved with sufficient funds. It is principally a matter of political policy as to whether these problems are addressed or not.

Several advantages of using a local examination rather than a national one have been identified. The flexibility amending the curriculum and exam simultaneously ensures maintenance of validity. An example of this flexibility occurred when the courses and exams were amended to reflect a change in the law concerning inclusion of a clause about water quality tests in purchase and sale contracts.

When item authors and panel reviewers fail to perceive latent ambiguities in test items, examinees have the opportunity to address their comments to the review panels. Then the review panels can change items where test-takers' comments present a convincing rationale.

Instructor performance was found to improve through feedback concerning student performance on particular portions of the examination. There are also advantages associated with the examination revenues remaining in the state and with the pride of ownership of the process.

There are disadvantages that accrue to a state-developed licensure examination. It must be recognized that economies of scale permit greater resources in terms of test development when a test is being used more widely than in only one state. The Maine real estate commission was willing to trade off the increased technical resources and resulting validity studies possible with a national examination for the locally devised, more subjectively valid test. The question can still be raised as to whether it is justifiable in time and effort to develop a local test rather than to use one which already has a track record.

Features of the Licensing System

Communication to the Field. Because a salesperson cannot complete a real estate transaction without the supervision of a broker, the requirement that brokers monitor the licensing process provides adequate system control. Each broker, for self-protection, will make certain that prospective salepersons have access to sales courses and licensure examination schedules.

Establishing the Schedule. The examination schedule is established and published sufficiently far in advance (generally at least one year) to allow any applicant to plan when to take the examination. An examination schedule must meet at least three criteria: (1) sufficient frequency to facilitate applicants' gaining access to the field without undue delay, (2) administration at least as often as courses are completed, and (3) permitting efficiency in terms of reasonable numbers of applicants.

The first and last criteria may result in some conflict. In a sparsely settled area, it is possible that only a very small number of applicants will be taking the examination over the period of a year. Yet the examination should not be delayed for so long that an applicant has to wait an undue length of time. A compromise must be provided to ensure that system efficiency is not totally sacrificed, yet the applicant is given as much consideration as possible.

Because the Maine application process includes completion of the three courses, examinations are scheduled immediately after the course ending dates as a minimum frequency.

Application Process. Licensure applicants must demonstrate their readiness for the final step for licensing. Within the Maine real estate system, this involves course completion or a valid out-of-state license, and experience, if appropriate (for example, sales experience for broker applicants).

The application process for most licensed professions often includes a standardized form that requires a relatively detailed description of the applicant's life. In instances such as real estate practice, a person's character is considered nearly as important as knowledge and skills. During the application process in Maine the candidate is reviewed for eligibility to take the examination. This review includes consideration of the life history and required references.

Relative to the schedule, the applicant should have the opportunity to take the examination promptly after application, to get the results, and to review the examination. Promptness in processing the application is a vital part of the entire system.

In general, the application process is centralized. This does not mean that only one location will offer the exam or review the results of the exam, but that one centralized facility should be reviewing the application, verifying its completeness, and scheduling the next step.

Receipt Control. Receipt control involves two distinct processes. The application must be controlled and maintained with some degree of confidentiality. Responsibility to the applicant demands that anything revealed on the application or the examination be used only as required to judge the fitness of the applicant for a license. The reception process also must include prompt notification of receipt of the application, when and where the applicant may participate in the next step in the process, and any other information necessary for the applicant to proceed in the licensing procedure.

The second control process is the security of the examination. Examination security is essential in order to have a valid examination. Security components can be grouped as on the following list:

- Item security (on a constant basis)
    - Item revisions
    - Care in storing and safeguarding
    - Limited access
- Examination security
    - Control during preparation, typing, and reproducing
    - Sequential numbering for receipt control
    - Limited access
    - Positive receipt control by maintaining a trail of access
    - Regular revision

- Control during/after administration
  Making sure that number of copies handed out and number returned are equal
  Collection of all scratch paper provided
  No interexaminee communication during administration

Constant vigilance must be maintained to ensure item security. Any person who has access to the items should meet all of the qualifications of a license holder and not be intending to apply for a license. There are two parts to an item, the stem and the response. If the keyed response can be maintained separate from the stem, the security issue becomes much less critical. Computerization of the examination items may either enhance or detract from the item security; it involves additional persons having access to items, but the computer can be used to separate correctly keyed responses from items.

A carefully maintained receipt control system and logging procedure may help to pinpoint when an examination has been compromised and to what extent that compromise has affected the validity of the examination. Furthermore, a properly maintained log of applicants is essential for ensuring that each applicant is given equal opportunity and equitable consideration.

Test Administration. A test cannot be considered valid if it has not been administered in exactly the same manner to every applicant. Validity therefore requires that three conditions be met: (1) There is a carefully prepared examination manual used by each administrator; (2) examination administrators are trained in using the standardized procedures; and (3) examinations at different locations are administered simultaneously.

Scoring the Examination. Most multiple-choice examinations have separate, machine-scorable answer sheets. As these answer sheets are part of the application process, they also must be strictly controlled. Even machine-scored answer sheets must be manually examined for stray marks or multiple responses. Important elements of scoring include promptness, care in safeguarding the confidentiality of the answer sheet, and accuracy.

Manual scoring requires double-checking. The importance of the results is such that every answer sheet should be scored twice. If the tests are machine scored, answer sheets should be scanned manually as previously discussed. Whether scored manually or by machine, it is important that the answer key be reviewed for proper keying of responses. Item analyses may aid in spotting poor questions or erroneously keyed responses which can then either be corrected or eliminated from scoring prior to reporting scores.

Record Review. Passing scores may be established as relative or fixed at a cut-off point. If the test score is the only criterion, the licensing decision is cut-and-dried. If performance, recommendations, or other factors are involved, each applicant's records must be examined. The applicant is entitled to know what has prevented him from being licensed.

Notification. The notification process to the applicant needs to provide at least:

- Acceptance or rejection notification
- If rejected, the appeal opportunities afforded the applicant
- The number correct or score for the examination and the relationship of this number to a passing score (for example, "Your score was 32 out of a possible 50 and the passing score was 35")
- Reasons for rejection

Candidate Feedback. Opportunity should be provided for post-test review by any candidate. Often this requirement is a legal right of the test-taker. Test items can be improved when the test-taker has the opportunity to explain why distractors have been selected rather than the keyed responses. Careful notes of these sessions should be maintained for at least two reasons: the possibility that legal action might be taken by the applicant, and, more importantly, the possibility of eliciting cues for improving the test.

Special System Requirements

Credibility. Many times a test may fail because the test-takers refuse to address it as a serious test or the users consider that it is not useful. A test may have very high marks for predictive, or concurrent, validity, but if there is no evidence that it deals with matters considered important to the test-takers and users, it will not be likely to serve the purpose intended. The Maine Board of Real Estate Commissioners was relatively satisfied with the national real estate examination published and scored by the Educational Testing Service (ETS). However, many of the real estate brokers and salespersons active in the state were not happy with the examination. Those teaching the courses for the commission felt that the test did not address the unique features of Maine real estate practice (Coit, 1979). As a result, the pressure placed on the board of commissioners persuaded them to discontinue the ETS examination in favor of one developed and administered by the Center for Real Estate Education at the University of Southern Maine. The issue was not strictly one of validity, but one of credibility. Credibility might be gauged from the answer to the question, "Do those taking the test believe that the test measures those aspects of the profession which are important to practitioners in the profession?"

Item Banking. Item banking, sometimes referred to loosely as item pooling, is the collection of a large set of test items and item characteristics from which the test maker may draw to construct each examination. In a sense, an item bank was developed in Maine for the real estate licensing examination —a sizable pool of items was collected, stored by topical area, and the item statistics recorded (for example, difficulty and discrimination). An attempt was made to develop this pool into a computerized item bank in order to use the computer for examination development and to enhance the parallelism of the examinations. A parallel test is one that has identical difficulty, discrimination, and variance. The more items can be specified with respect to parallel difficulty and discrimination, the more likely it is that items will be selected to produce tests comparable to previous ones.

Item banking requires that one first determine the important criteria for selecting an item for the examination, code the criteria, and then set up detailed procedures for entry of the items and revisions, for retrieval of the items, and for publishing the test. During this test-generation process, the issues of security and control must be addressed. A typical item bank minimally contains for each item data on type of item, validity coefficient, reliability coefficient, difficulty level, item author and reviewer, date of origin and review, source of item, and history of item usage.

If these data are all included, only those which are selection criteria need to be coded to aid in the computerized selection—this would generally be the item analysis statistics. Though the goal of establishing a computerized item bank was not realized for the Maine real estate exam because of lack of funding, the idea has not been entirely abandoned.

System Updating. There is a need to continually update the system. Not only must test items be constantly reviewed for possible changes in practice or law, but advances in test methodology need to be considered. Some important aspects of updating include: changes in practice within the profession; rewriting of items for achieving better discrimination; revision of the table of specifications for the test to better meet domain samples; and consideration of more efficient methods of measurement, for example, computerized test taking, item sampling, and so on.

Continuing Research. Updating the system is based on varying sources of input. One of the more significant is continuing research on the test. It is imperative that items be analyzed constantly and that reliability be checked each time the test is administered. Continuing attempts should be made to establish the validity of the examination. Determination of predictive validity requires substantial investments of time, money, and professional dedication. In the long run, such studies are extremely beneficial. Validity is a relative matter and can only be approximated or estimated. Continued research in the area of validity is critical to a well-respected licensing examination.

A certain proportion of the revenue for administering licensing examination should regularly be set aside for research. Some examples of important research areas include: validity studies—predictive, concurrent, content (from job analyses); item analyses—item-descriptive characteristics, validity, and so on; more efficient testing methodology (item sampling and computerized item stems and responses); better documentation of test specifications; and review of potential item or examination biases.

Summary

Although national examinations can provide a state agency with savings in regard to test development and maintenance and can supply assurance of a quality test, local conditions may dictate that the licensing agency develop and maintain its own test. Such was the case for Maine. This case study presents an overview of the steps required to operate and maintain the examination component of a licensing system. Test security, receipt control of applications, communication with candidates, scheduling examination administration, and record keeping are important considerations in the maintenance of the system. In addition to these important considerations, continued study of test performance can lead to the improvement of the test and the examination process.

References

Coit, C. S. "Administration of a Local Licensure Examination: The Maine Experience." Paper presented at annual meeting of the National Council on Measurement in Education, San Francisco, April 1979.

Cromack, T. R. "Characteristics of a Locally Developed Licensure Examination." Paper presented at annual meeting of the National Council on Measurement in Education, San Francisco, April 1979.

8

Army Programs for Certifying Skills

Linda J. Schultz-Shiner
Rebecca L. Oxford-Carpenter

A discussion of military practices regarding occupational licensing provides an interesting dimension to this volume. This chapter presents a description of some of the main programs in the U.S. Army that focus on skills certification. In the military, certification of skills can be seen as the analogue to occupational licensing. In many areas reciprocity agreements exist between the military and licensure agencies. It should be noted that all of the services—Navy, Army, Air Force, and Marines—engage in some form of skills certification. Discussion in this chapter is limited to Army practices. Furthermore, the emphasis is on Army skills certification practices that relate to enlisted personnel rather than to commissioned officers, because enlisted personnel make up the majority of the Army population and are frequently involved in skills certification programs. Unlike officer programs, certification programs for enlisted personnel (with the exception of the non-commissioned officer academies) deal primarily with trade occupations. In contrast, many programs for non-commissioned and commissioned officers focus on the development of managerial and leadership skills. This chapter includes a discussion of various Army Continuing Education System (ACES) programs, job training programs given before and after soldiers enter their units, and special skills proficiency testing programs.

ACES Programs

The Army Continuing Education System (ACES) is a worldwide agency of the U.S. Army that offers many educational opportunities to soldiers for obtaining skills certification. Some relevant ACES programs are described in the following sections.

Servicemembers Opportunity Colleges Associate Degree. One ACES program is the Servicemembers Opportunity Colleges Associate Degree (SOCAD) program established in 1972. This program is designed to provide opportunities to a servicemember to earn college credits for skills and knowledge acquired in the Army and to obtain an associate degree in any one of a variety of fields corresponding to the individual's military occupational specialty (MOS). Although the program focus is on the educational needs of the Army, the program is structured so that it can be adapted to the other services. Enlisted personnel, particularly non-commissioned officers, comprise the target population for the SOCAD program. More than 400 postsecondary institutions offer SOCAD courses for military personnel (Servicemembers Opportunity Colleges, 1981).

Instruction via flexible curricula takes place during off-duty hours and may be given on the military installation, at an easily accessible campus site, or through some "nontraditional" means such as correspondence, television, or independent study courses. The program is sponsored primarily by the American Association of State Colleges and Universities and the American Association of Community and Junior Colleges, along with all other cooperating agencies and the military services.

The SOCAD program concentrates chiefly on job-related areas. In fact, the degree can be awarded for demonstrated skills proficiency on the job. The American Council on Education has developed a *Guide to the Evaluation of Educational Experiences in the Armed Services,* which is used to assess military job experiences for the purpose of recommending college credit by a college or university. Currently associate degrees may be earned in the following job-related fields: accounting, automotive maintenance, aviation maintenance, communications electronics, computer maintenance, construction, data processing, diesel maintenance, digital electronics, food service management, law enforcement services, management science, medical records, office management, and transportation technology. Also there is a flexible curriculum including general studies and liberal arts. Credit for skills and experience may also be applied toward a four-year college degree. (Servicemembers Opportunity Colleges, 1981; Education Program Administrator, The Adjutant General's Office, personal communication, February 23, 1984).

The SOCAD program is especially advantageous because it offers a systematic approach toward obtaining a college degree which can be coordinated with the normal rotation of Army assignments. Moreover, the Army will pay for 75 to 90 percent of the individual's tuition. Attainment of a degree, through the SOCAD program serves as a means of certification of job skills proficiency. More than 250,000 military students participate annually in the SOCAD program (Servicemembers Opportunity Colleges, 1981). Automatic transfer of college degree credits among the colleges within the network is guaranteed in each curriculum area.

Army Apprenticeship Program. The Army Apprenticeship Program (AAP) provides Army enlisted personnel the opportunity to document work experience and to earn an apprenticeship certificate in a particular skill area at no cost to the individual. The interested soldier registers for the program through the Education Center, which verifies eligibility. While the individual trains in his or her skill area, careful logging of hours is maintained. For most apprenticeships, 2,000 to 8,000 hours must be logged and supported by proper documentation in order to attain the status of journeyworker. A number of hours of formal education are also usually required as part of the program. The Department of Labor, which acts as the certifying agency for the numerous trade organizations that register with it, awards a Certificate of Completion of Apprenticeship to the soldier. The certificate acknowledges that the soldier is a skilled professional in the specific field of the apprenticeship. Civilian employers widely recognize the certificate, which thus facilitates transition to the civilian work force for the soldier who leaves the military. Some of the technical areas in which it is possible to obtain an apprenticeship certificate include air defense, armor, artillery, communications, engineering, intelligence, ordnance, and transportation (Department of the Army, 1982a). Approximately 50,000 soldiers have entered the program since it began in 1973, and between 27,000 and 28,000 are currently enrolled (Education Program Administrator, The Adjutant General's office, personal communication, January 17, 1984). Because the AAP involves a lengthy process (it could take up to six years to complete), the number of soldiers who actually finish the program is relatively small. For example, 210 soldiers had completed apprenticeship as of December 1981 (Mouze, 1981).

Defense Activity for Non-Traditional Education Support. The Defense Activity for Non-Traditional Education Support (DANTES) has replaced the U.S. Armed Forces Institute (USAFI) as the contracting agent for civilian licensing in numerous technical areas. DANTES was established by Congress in 1974 to provide independent study and examination programs for military personnel (Goldberg, 1977). The soldier who desires to receive a civilian professional license or certification contacts his or her Army Education Center, which then obtains the appropriate examination through DANTES. A sampling of some of the professional organizations which offer licensing or certification examinations through DANTES include the American Association of Medical Assistants, American Medical Technologists, the Institute for the Certification of Engineering Technicians, and, perhaps the most popular one, the National Institute for Automotive Service Excellence.

In addition to licensing examinations, DANTES also provides college examinations, such as those from the American College Testing and Assessment Program. DANTES also handles the General Educational Development (GED) examination for troops stationed overseas and recommends college credit through DANTES Subject Standardized Tests. Soldiers must pay fees associated with certification tests given through DANTES (Department of Defense, 1980; Education Program Administrator, The Adjutant General's Office, personal communication, January 17, 1984).

High School Completion Program. The High School Completion (HSC) program gives soldiers the opportunity to complete their high school educations through either of two routes: first, taking courses and receiving a regular diploma or second, taking the GED examination and receiving a state-issued certificate. The first route involves completing courses taught at a regionally accredited high school during off-duty hours. In the second, the GED certificate is issued by the state in which the soldier is stationed, with different states having different passing scores. Soldiers may take the GED after completing courses in the Army Basic Skills Education Program. During fiscal year 1983, 3,725 soldiers received high school diplomas, and 12,990 received GED certification through the ACES program (Education Program Administrator, The Adjutant General's Office, personal communication, January 17, 1984).

Registry Transcript System. The new Army/American Council on Education Registry Transcript System (AARTS) is a computerized system designed to record officially soldier's military training, experience, and standardized test scores in one easily accessible document. The concept was initiated by the Office of the Adjutant General, and the Training and Doctrine Command will implement the system. A three- to five-year phase-in is projected from the 1983 inception. This centralized record will be advantageous both to the individual and to the Army as a whole (Education Program Administrator, The Adjutant General's Office, personal communication, January 17, 1984).

Other ACES Programs. In addition to the programs already discussed, noncredit programs also exist that provide certificates to soldiers who take technical or trade courses at accredited educational institutions. For example, a soldier who takes a masonry course can receive a certificate of completion that is presentable to future employers.

We have discussed a number of Army education programs

that provide certification and licensing. Now we will turn to job training programs occurring before soldiers enter their units and providing various types of certification.

Pre-Unit Job Training Programs

Job training is first provided to the soldier in Advanced Individual Training (AIT), which takes place immediately after Basic Training but before the soldier begins actual job duties in his or her unit in "permanent party" status. AIT results in the awarding of a military occupational specialty designation (MOS) and in presentation of a certificate of job training course completion. In some MOSs, the certificate of completion indicates "recommended (college) credits" for completion of the course and awarding of the MOS (The Adjutant General's Office, personal communication, January 17, 1984).

The training development model used for AIT in the Army, as well as in job training in the other three armed forces, is the Instructional Systems Development (ISD) model. This model was first described in depth in TRADOC Pamphlet 350-30 (Department of the Army, 1975) for the Army and NAVEDTRA 106A (Department of the Navy, 1975) for the Navy. A revision under TRADOC Regulation 350-7 entitled *A Systems Approach to Training* (Department of the Army, 1982b) preserves the ISD procedure while providing for greater flexibility to schools for implementation. As a consequence, it is possible that training schools may demonstrate a renewed interest in implementing the ISD model more systematically than they are currently implementing it.

ISD evolved out of operations analysis concepts of World War II. The model is a result of two factors: a recognition that the future would demand increasingly large pools of well-trained military personnel in highly technical areas and a reaction against conventional, unsystematic training techniques. ISD was originally intended to be a means of designing training that would optimize total system effectiveness, maximize efficiency within the training subsystem, ensure that training is relevant to the job, and reflect modern training technology. In their evaluation of the current implementation of the ISD model across the four services, Vineberg and Joyner (1980) determined that ISD was not meeting some of its original intents for a number of technical and operational reasons. However, ISD is an important move toward making training development more rational and systematic, although the actual implementation falls short of the theory.

The five typical phases of the ISD model are analyzing the job (known as "front-end analysis"), developing objectives and tests, specifying learning activities/events, implementing the instructional management plan, and conducting internal and external evaluations for system revision. Although the ISD model emerged about the same time as the national trend toward criterion-referenced testing and associated techniques (such as individualization, self-pacing, computer-assisted instruction, and computer-managed instruction), ISD should not be considered synonymous with those techniques. Rather, ISD is primarily a *process* through which training alternatives are selected rather than a set of specific training strategies or products. However, in practice ISD clearly implies the use of instructional methodologies and criterion-referenced tests that emphasize individualization, because front-end job analysis and development of objectives are designed to determine and specify adequate on-the-job performance—the criterion toward which the training moves.

Several investigations have been conducted on the type of measurement used in Army job training. Swezey, Pearlstein, and Ton (1975) examined testing practices in Army training schools, training centers, and extension courses. In interviewing 105 training and testing personnel, these researchers found that the primary use of test results was to evaluate soldier skill performance. At that time, approximately a decade ago, job training tests were mostly nonstandardized, multiple-choice, paper-and-pencil, and norm-referenced. However, criterion-referenced tests were beginning to spark interest because of their capability to measure an individual's performance in reference to a specific skill standard rather than in reference to performance of a norm group.

Likewise, Vineberg and Joyner (1983) made some helpful generalizations about the military job training measurement system as they had known it over several decades. They stated that job training measurement is the most frequent type of individual performance assessment used in the military and that achievement testing in military job training schools was accomplished mainly through paper-and-pencil, multiple-choice tests of information recall. Hands-on testing was used in certain occupations, such as those of rifleman, pilot, and air traffic controller, but was not widely employed.

A more recent investigation of Army job training measurement (Oxford-Carpenter and others, 1984) covering eleven courses found several new trends. First, criterion-referenced tests were now typical in Army job training schools at the AIT level. Second, there was extensive use of hands-on testing for training in most courses. However, training courses, which had been far more self-paced in recent years, were now back in the group-paced or lock-step mode. An internal philosophical and instructional contradiction may exist when a system simultaneously uses criterion-referenced testing and lock-step or group-paced instruction instead of self-pacing.

In terms of current AIT testing, it was found that trainees were expected to achieve competency cumulatively throughout a given course (Oxford-Carpenter and others, 1984). That means that trainees were expected to pass successively all of the tests given. However, "No-Go" on hands-on tests and failing grades on written tests were treated very differently from course to course and from school to school. Officially, only two retests were permitted in most courses, but in practice more were sometimes given. If, for example, the failure was slight or based on a misunderstanding, or if the trainee had a superior previous record, additional testing might be allowed. Trainers and testers made every effort to see that each trainee passed the course. All tests were monitored to prevent cheating. Prompting was almost irrelevant because in many instances the trainee had a training manual available during testing.

Testing practices were not standardized within courses across installations, according to the 1984 study. In other words, two courses for the same job taught at different installations sometimes used different testing practices. Furthermore, training content was sometimes different for "twin" courses for the same MOS as instructed at different training schools. These findings on nonstandardization supported those of Swezey, Pearlstein, and Ton (1975) a decade earlier.

In this section we have discussed job training programs that occur before the soldier is sent to his or her first job. The next section explains certification in a series of resident training programs for enlisted personnel.

Non-Commissioned Officer Education System

The Army has a Non-Commissioned Officer Education System (NCOES) for soldiers in grades E3 through E9. NCOES is an integrated system of resident training, supervised on-the-job training, self-study, and on-the-job experience for non-commissioned officers (NCOs) and specialists throughout their careers. Upon completion of any level of NCOES, the soldier is awarded a certificate of completion and a diploma (The Adjutant General's Office, personal communication, January 17, 1984). Courses are given at four levels: primary, basic, advanced, and senior (Schaefer, 1983). These levels are geared to specific Army pay grades and skill levels. Grades E4 and below are known as skill level 1; grade E5 refers to skill level 2; grade E6 is keyed to skill level 3; grade E7 is linked with skill level 4; and grades E8 and E9 are related to skill level 5. Army grades begin at E1.

The Primary NCO Course (PNCOC) for combat arms is a non-MOS-specific, field-oriented course to teach soldiers relevant skills and tasks, including leadership. It is conducted at NCO academies with a first priority given to grade E5 soldiers and a second priority to grade E4 and E3 soldiers. The Primary Technical Course (PTC) provides MOS training at Army skill level 2 with first priority given to soldiers in or selected for promotion to grade E5. PTC is taught at Army service schools. The Primary Leadership Course (PLC) is given at NCO academies and covers leadership, supervision, and management. Soldiers in grades E5, E4, and E3 in leadership positions are eligible.

The Basic NCO Course (BNCOC) for combat arms stresses

performance-oriented training techniques for specified MOS. Conducted at NCO academies, this course gives first priority to soldiers selected for E6. The Basic Technical Course (BTC) focuses on critical tasks at the Army skill level 3 for given MOSs. Again, E6 selectees are first priority for this course, which is conducted at service schools. At the basic level and higher, no specifically leadership-oriented courses are given.

The next level offers the Advanced NCO Course (ANCOC), which emphasizes MOS-related tasks at grade E7. It is conducted at service schools but can also be taken by extension course. ANCOC is limited in attendance to soldiers in grades E6 and E7. A Department of the Army selection board selects attendees.

Two courses are taught at the senior level: the First Sergeant Course (ISG Course) and the Sergeants Major Academy (USASMA). The First Sergeant Course stresses training in the most critical tasks in the duty position of first sergeant. No priority is given to MOS. This course is conducted at Ft. Bliss, Texas, with attendees selected by Major Commands according to quotas established by the Department of the Army. Participants must be in grade E8, E7, or E7 (promotable) and be selected to fill a first sergeant position. The Sergeants Major Academy trains selected soldiers for positions of highest responsibility. There is no MOS priority. This course is also conducted at Ft. Bliss, although a nonresident course is also offered. Participants are chosen by a Department of the Army board and are in grades E8 and E9 with less than twenty-three years of service.

NCOES levels are attained within three weeks to six months. NCOES is administered by the Department of the Army. ACES will soon begin providing diagnostic testing in basic skills to NCOES selectees. Those who do not pass the test will attend classes for basic skills remediation before entering the appropriate NCOES level.

Skill Qualification Test

The Army's Skill Qualification Test (SQT) program was originally designed as a criterion-referenced, performance-oriented assessment program. It was conceived in 1974 and implemented in 1977 to measure proficiency, identify weaknesses, and improve performance with respect to combat readiness and skill on the job. This program was in effect from 1977 until November 1983, at which time regulations supporting a change in approach became effective. The purpose of this section is to outline the development of the SQT program and to show the changing trends in Army proficiency testing.

The SQT served to decentralize the training process by transferring many of the training responsibilities from the schools and centers to the units. In addition, SQT results ultimately figured in individual considerations for promotion of soldiers in grades E4 and E5 and still do (Army Research Institute, personal communication, January 12, 1984). The SQT emphasized skill mastery and provided the basis for a "Go/No-Go" decision for individual soldiers.

Other services also administer tests of proficiency, for example, the Air Force Specialty Knowledge tests and Promotion Fitness examinations and the Navy's examination for advancement, which is part of the Navy Enlisted Advancement System. However, the Army is the only service which has attempted to provide standardized, hands-on proficiency tests on a service-wide basis (Vineberg and Joyner, 1983).

For each MOS and skill level, a Soldiers Manual (SM) was to be developed in accordance with the ISD model described earlier. Each SM presented a clear statement of tasks, behaviors, conditions, and standards that the soldier was expected to follow and master. SQT items were to be developed from the information in the manuals.

The goal was to develop a SQT for every MOS in the Army. However, as of fiscal year 1981 the SQT had been developed for approximately 200 of the 351 occupational specialties. For the low-density MOSs, it was determined that the development of MOS-specific SQTs was not feasible, and common-task tests (CTT) were administered instead (U.S. General Accounting Office, 1982).

SQT development for annual administration by MOS and skill level was a fifteen-month cyclic process. Each SQT was allowed to be administered only during a specifically designated "test window" period not exceeding nine months. Each post determined the time(s) within an SQT window during which a particular test was administered. After expiration, old SQT versions gave way to new ones (U.S. General Accounting Office, 1982).

The SQT was generally composed of three parts: (1) the skill component, which was a multiple-choice, paper-and-pencil test intended to evaluate the ability to apply knowledge necessary to perform a task; (2) the hands-on component, in which a soldier actually performed selected tasks in a controlled, standardized setting; and (3) the job-site component, administered by the soldier's immediate supervisor in his or her own job setting and made up of hands-on tests (U.S. General Accounting Office, 1982).

The hands-on and job-site components differed in two ways. First, the hands-on component was administered by a testing team at a centralized site, while the job-site component was administered by the incumbent's own supervisor. Second, the hands-on component was standardized, while the job-site component was not.

A fourth component that was sometimes used was the "alternate" hands-on component, consisting of a written test intended to substitute for the hands-on test in situations where the facilities and equipment necessary for the hands-on test were not available.

Different samples of tasks from each MOS were selected yearly for the SQT using criteria established by the Army Training and Doctrine Command. A subset of no more than thirty-five tasks comprised the SQT. This number is small compared to the total number of tasks a soldier was required to know—the SQT tested approximately 25 percent of the skills critical to any given job (U.S. General Accounting Office, 1982).

A standard SQT procedure included the formal notification to the soldier of the upcoming test administration, up to sixty days in advance. This notice told the soldier exactly which tasks would be tested. The soldier then received a varied amount of training on the selected tasks, depending on MOS, availability of trainers, other duties, and local command emphasis. Additionally, soldiers were permitted a "dry run" on the hands-on component using the test equipment and were encouraged to practice any tasks on which deficient skills were exhibited before the actual testing.

Some problems surfaced in the SQT program: expense of time and resources, difficulty in providing test developers with feedback from the previous year's test in time for them to develop new tests, subjectivity in job-site testing, possible validity problems, and inequities in the use of SQT results in promotion decisions (U.S. General Accounting Office, 1982). As a result of these problems, the Army decided to modify its proficiency testing program. The new version is described in the next section.

Individual Training Evaluation Program

Although the SQT program was based on sound theory, its implementation problems caused the Army to reconsider the way job skills proficiency could be tested. The product of this reconsideration was the Army Individual Training Evaluation Program (ITEP), implemented in November 1983 under Army Regulation 350-37. The ITEP contains three primary methods of evaluation: the commander's evaluation, the common-task test (CTT), and a new type of SQT. The old SQT had proved valuable as a training evaluation and personnel management tool (Bolin, 1981) and thus was revised for incorporation into the new approach.

The commander's evaluation is executed through a checklist procedure. Soldiers Manual tasks listed in a Job Book are tested and then rated Go or No-Go.

The CTT is principally a hands-on test administered by the unit commander to evaluate proficiency on common soldier tasks. However, as with the hands-on component of the old SQT, a written test is provided when equipment is unavailable.

The SQT portion of the ITEP is now solely a written test developed by MOS proponent schools. Items still are based on a subset of MOS skill level Soldiers Manual tasks.

By the use of these measures, the Army hopes to alleviate some of the problems associated with the former SQT program and to increase the fidelity of the tests. It is too early to assess the success of the ITEP.

Further Investigation

This chapter has discussed a number of programs for skill certification in the Army. These are some of the key programs, but they are not the only ones offered by the Army. There is clearly a wide range of opportunities for certification—and in some cases civilian licensing—available to Army enlisted personnel. Other military services also have extensive enlisted personnel certification programs of various types. Officer certification programs are another dimension, which has not been discussed here. Many of these programs involve testing and competency issues, such as establishment of proficiency standards and use of tests to affect career decisions. Because of the prevalence of military certification programs and the many interesting issues involved, this subject deserves further research attention, not only in the Army but also in the other military services.

The sophisticated certification programs of the British and German armies could be considered as possible models for the further development of skill certification programs in the U.S. military. The British army offers a systematic program of "transition training" for soldiers leaving the army to certify the skills they have obtained while in the service. The German army has a "subscription service" in which already certified civilians, such as highly skilled mechanics, are brought into the army for two years and then recertified before being sent back to private industry (Army Research Institute, personal communication, January 10, 1984).

Clearly the field of military job skills certification is ripe for further investigation, from both the theoretical and the operational viewpoints. Effects of certification on the individual and on the system are profound in many cases.

References

American Council on Education. *Guide to the Evaluation of Educational Experiences in the Armed Services.* Washington, D.C.: American Council on Education, 1982.

Blanchard, B. "Army Apprenticeship Smooths Civilian Work Path." *Pentagram,* 1984, *31,* 41.

Bolin, S. F. "A Task-Based Approach to Soldier Training." *Defense Management Journal,* 1981, *9,* 24-28.

Department of Defense. *DANTES Examination Program Handbook* (DOD 1322.8-H). Washington, D.C.: Department of Defense, 1980.

Department of the Army. *Interservice Procedures for Instructional Systems Development* (TRADOC Pam. 350-30). Washington, D.C.: Department of the Army, 1975.

Department of the Army. *The Army Apprenticeship Program: Learn a Valuable Skill and Earn a Certificate to Document It.* Washington, D.C.: U.S. Government Printing Office, 1982a.

Department of the Army. *A Systems Approach to Training* (TRADOC Reg. 350-7). Washington, D.C.: Department of the Army, 1982b.

Department of the Army. *Army Individual Training and Evaluation Program* (Army Reg. 350-37). Washington, D.C.: Department of the Army, 1983.

Department of the Navy. *Interservice Procedures for Instructional Systems Development* (NAVEDTRA 106A). Washington, D.C.: Department of the Navy, 1975.

Goldberg, R. G. "Certification and Licensure Programs for Occupational Skill Documentation." Paper presented at the 19th annual conference of the Military Testing Association, San Antonio, Tex., Oct. 1977.

Mouze, V. "Army Apprenticeship Program: A Way to Get Ahead." *Soldiers,* 1981, *36,* 11-13.

Oxford-Carpenter, R. L., and others. "Training Development and Testing Practices in Army Job Training." Paper presented at the annual meeting of the American Educational Research Association, New Orleans, La., April 1984.

Schaefer, T. "Memorandum of June 10, 1983. Subject: NCOES, Army Reg. 351-1." Alexandria, Va.: Office of the Adjutant General, 1983.

Servicemembers Opportunity Colleges. *Servicemembers Opportunity Colleges Associate Degree Program for Military Personnel.* Washington, D.C.: Servicemembers Opportunity Colleges, 1981.

Swezey, R. W., Pearlstein, R. B., and Ton, W. H. *Criterion-Referenced Testing: A Discussion of Theory and Practice in the Army* (Research Memorandum 75-11). Alexandria, Va.: U.S. Army Research Institute for the Behavioral and Social Sciences, 1975.

U.S. General Accounting Office. *The Army Needs to Modify Its System for Measuring Individual Soldier Proficiency.* Washington, D.C.: U.S. General Accounting Office, 1982.

Vineberg, R., and Joyner, J. N. *Instructional Systems Development (ISD) in the Armed Services: Methodology and Application* (Contract No. MDA 903-77-C-0335). Alexandria, Va.: Human Resources Research Organization, 1980.

Vineberg, R., and Joyner, J. N. "Performance Measurement in the Military Services." In F. Landy, S. Zedeck, and J. Cleveland (Eds.), *Performance Measurement and Theory.* Hillsdale, N.J.: Erlbaum, 1983.

9

A Systems Approach to Studying Licensing

Stephanie R. Blecharczyk
Jim C. Fortune

As has been stated by writers of previous chapters, licensing is here to stay, and testing, whether it be for skills, knowledge, or abilities, is an inherent part of the process. This applies both to private and public sector occupations, and it is perhaps the measurement aspect of testing that establishes the need to look at the generic process of licensing.

In the first chapter Shimberg reviews briefly the evolution of occupational licensing in our society. This review portrays occupational licensing as: (1) a practice that in the last century has grown from regulation of a handful of professions to regulation of more than 800 occupations and professions, (2) a practice in which several issues and areas of controversy persist, and (3) a practice which is coming under increased public scrutiny.

The focus of the second, third, and fourth chapters is testing. Burns describes the process; Kane focuses upon the issue that has received the most press—test validity; and Impara and Stoker address both validity and reliability from a measurement perspective. Vertiz overviews legal precedents for licensing, established through judicial cases. Case studies serve to illustrate the individuality and variance in the practice of licensing.

Yet, there are important consistencies in the practice of licensing, including authorization, function, and key components.

Rationale for the Concept of Licensing as a System

Until the late 1960s, interest in occupational licensing as a generic process was almost nonexistent (Shimberg, Esser, and Kruger, 1972). Of course, there was interest on the part of practitioners within the licensed occupations, but the principles and practice of the generic process were not subjected to public concern, evaluative analysis, or research investigation. Social concerns such as civil rights, unemployment, a depressed economy, and an expanding bureaucracy have enhanced the visibility of issues. With this new visibility, knowledge of the generality of relationships in the generic process of occupational licensing has become more important to developers of new licensing programs, to reformers of existing programs, and to consulting methodologists.

Systems analysis has been shown useful in the development of conceptual frameworks for research (Gagne, 1962), in the design of training programs (Miller, 1962) and in the development of evaluative paradigms (Kronenberg, Rogers, and Greene, 1980). This approach, through an analysis of component variations, functional interrelationships, and systems requirements, permits the identification of types or models within a system. From the output of the systems analysis, paradigms depicting conceptual frameworks can be developed for each type. The purpose of this chapter is to explore the usefulness of the systems analysis approach in depicting the generic process of occupational licensing.

Generally, a system can be thought of as a set or arrangement of procedures and components organized to perform a function or accomplish a repetitious task. This set or arrangement becomes a system when its components and procedures become so interrelated or connected that they form a unified, organized whole. Although there may be variations in the interrelationships and in the selection and sequence of procedures and components, a system performs in a generic way, permitting a meaningful general discussion of system requirements and principles.

Occupational licensing programs satisfy the definition of a system. The function of the occupational licensing system is to safeguard public health, safety, and welfare from potential harm which may ensue from incompetent practice of the regulated occupation. This protection is achieved through regulation of entry into the occupation, through the establishment of standards of safe practice, and through the disciplining of those who do not adhere to the standards. Table 1 shows the steps that occur in the establishment of a licensing program.

Table 1. Steps Involved in the Establishment of an Occupational Licensing Program

Step No.	*Activity*
1	A potential threat from incompetent, dishonest, or irresponsible practice of an occupation to public health, safety, or welfare is identified.
2	A statute or a mandate to regulate the occupation is drafted into legislation.
3	This licensing mandate is passed into law by the legislation.
4	A regulatory agency or a professional board is created and staffed.
5	The agency or board establishes, according to the law, rules, regulations, and policies and develops a record system for the licensing process.
6	A set of minimum entry standards deemed necessary for competent practice is established (usually through task analysis).

Occupational licensing systems are made up of several components that work in concert to permit review of qualifications of applicants to the licensed occupation and, if these qualifications are satisfactory, to issue licenses. Table 2 delineates steps involved in the operation of an occupational licensing program.

Components of the Licensing System

From a review of tables 1 and 2, components of the licensing system can be identified. Note that the components can

Table 2. Steps Involved in the Operation of an Occupational Licensing Program

Step No.	*Activity*
1	The board identifies evidences (usually a test is developed) of minimum standards that it can review for the ascertainment of qualification.
2	An application procedure is designed, and criteria for eligibility for application are published.
3	Applications are received.
4	Evidence of candidate qualifications is received.
5	Applications and evidence are reviewed, and decisions for licensing are made.
6	Applicants are notified of results of the review, and licenses are awarded to successful applicants.
7	A review, follow up, or evaluation of the licensing decisions is conducted periodically.
8	Licensees are monitored. (Investigations of reported violations are made.)
9	Enforcement of the mandate is enacted. (Prosecution of violations or revocation of licenses occurs.)

be anchored either to persons or documents defining the system. In this analysis we prefer to identify components by the documentation that defines and structures licensing activities. Under this scheme of component identification, persons involved in the system are considered controlled by the documentation. They implement activities specified by the documents and serve to blend these documents into a unity that defines the system.

Components of the licensing system are (1) regulation statute or licensing mandate; (2) administration, including agency or board specifications, rules, regulations, policies, and recordkeeping procedures; (3) specifications and documentation of the minimum entry standards; (4) application and application control procedures; (5) review procedures; and (6) procedures for monitoring practice in the occupation and for enforcement of standards.

Legislative Authority for Regulation of an Occupation. Regulation of an occupation is implemented only after authorizing legislation has been written and enacted. This legislation is based on protection of public health, welfare, and safety. Documentation of the threat to the public represents the basis for establishment of legal authority to regulate an occupation. The threat may be identified in several ways.

Shimberg, Esser and Kruger (1972) discuss the legislative process that is most frequently followed. "Although the rhetoric of licensing places much emphasis on protecting the public health and safety, in practice the public has little to say about enacting licensing legislation. The sponsoring group usually drafts the legislation and then has it introduced by a friendly legislator. Members and friends participate in an organized letter-writing campaign to support the legislation; practitioners and paid lobbyists call on legislators in person to obtain commitments for the law. When the hearings are held, expert witnesses can be summoned to lend their prestige and technical knowledge to the legislative effort. The public is all but forgotten. Concerned citizens who may be opposed to the legislation rarely have the financial resources to initiate a counter-campaign. Thus, legislators are likely to hear only one side of the issue and to mistake a lack of opposition for tacit assent on the part of the public" (p. 14).

The nature of the public threat may differ in regard to the intensity, scope, and urgency of the peril. These differences appear to be related to the nature of the occupation and type of public services performed. Scope of the threat to some degree determines the level of government at which the regulatory agency or legislation is located. Federal regulation tends to involve transportation and communication, both of which have interstate dimensions. Other instances of federal regulation are in industries such as the nuclear power industry. These instances can be justified by both the intensity and urgency of the threat. Authority for regulation of other occupations rests at the state level; however, licensing may be deferred to a smaller unit of government such as a city or county.

The jurisdiction of licensing at the federal, state, or local levels is congruent with the governmental unit issuing the regulation legislation. Both state and local licensing may involve reciprocity across governmental units. However, reciprocity agreements are not as commonplace as might be expected. Regulation and, consequently, licensing at the federal level are administered by a regulatory agency. Most regulation and licensing at state and local levels are administered by licensing boards.

Issues that persist in regard to legislation are absence of public voice in the process, low mobility and absence of reciprocity in some occupations, and enactment of nonessential regulatory legislation. Arguments for increased public voice point out that regulation of many occupations begins with incumbents in the occupation who wish to limit the number of practitioners and raise costs of services. Similar arguments are made concerning reciprocity.

Administrative Procedures. The licensing board or administering agency is charged with implementation of the law. From the law administrators develop rules, regulations, and policies which will govern the licensing operation. Many of the rules and regulations are taken directly from the law: reciprocity, fee structure, terms of office, lines of authority, and requirements for application. The local board or agency personnel specify meeting protocol, security procedures, schedule or calendar, the specifics of the record-keeping system, and other operational procedures, such as the handling and control of applications, appeals processes, and interaction with other governance agencies.

Generally, state board members are appointed by the governor, and federal agency personnel are handled through appointments within the civil service system. In almost all cases administrative personnel come from the regulated occupation. Administration of licensing programs varies in regard to autonomy: Some units operate without other agency supervision, some units are required to report to another agency, and some are under direct administrative control of another agency. Shimberg (1980) identified five types of licensing boards according to degrees of autonomy.

Minimum Entry Standards. There are two types of requirements for occupational licensure. One concerns eligibility for applying. These requirements frequently include minimum years of schooling, citizenship, local residence, experience in the occupation, and training in a specific program. Although it is difficult to see how years of schooling, citizenship, and local residence are related to performance in some licensed occupations, precedents for retaining these requirements have been established. In some cases, courts have disallowed the use of one or more of these traditional requirements. (See Chapter Five on judicial cases.) The experience and participation required in a given training program are interrelated, in that apprenticeship provides both in some occupations. Type of occupation does not appear related to either experience or number of years required (Shimberg, 1980). In some occupations, training programs are designed to address directly the licensing requirements, so specific training experience may be required.

The second group of requirements addresses the candidate's qualifications in the occupational area. Readiness for entry includes two major considerations: minimum levels of knowledge, skills, and abilities (KSAs) and an indication that the candidate possesses the "good character" required in practice.

Generally, task or job analysis is the most acceptable method for identifying and documenting the knowledge, skills, and abilities required for entry. Several methods besides task analysis have been used in the past, but these methods lack both objectivity, or independence from incumbent judgment, and thoroughness. Among these unsatisfactory methods are logical extrapolation, which fails to identify any except the obvious requirements; surveys of incumbents, which may lack objectivity; and conceptual analyses of training programs, which do not establish direct links with job performance. Task or job analysis is actually a family of research techniques employed to build objective descriptions of job requirements. Job analysis strategy is to observe directly the conduct of a job and list each step required to complete the tasks. The observation process can take the form of any of several methods of observation or objective data collection. One of the most frequently used methods is actual shadowing, or on-the-job observation. A second method is collection of data through critical incidents. Variations may include the analysis of documents describing work functions and responsibilities. Still another option is the triangularization of job descriptions gained from incumbents and supervisors with observation information. Observations may be expanded or verified through interviews with practitioners in the occupation.

In the identification of required knowledge, skills, and abilities, care must be taken that the KSAs identified are entry-level rather than those developed through on-the-job experience. The KSAs identified for licensing should be only those required to protect the public and not those associated with excellence in practice. The documentation of minimum qualifications for safe practice is the major consideration in licensing. Evidence to be presented by a candidate as determined by the licensing board or administrative agency may include documentation of the completion of training, satisfactory performance on a licensing test, and completion of a residency or apprenticeship. Documentation of training is usually required when minimum entry standards are linked directly to specific training. For the occupations where this linkage exists, instructors frequently supply transcripts of the applicant's performance and program content.

One almost universal evidence required in licensing decisions is applicant performance on a standardized test. Usually the nature of the required KSAs plays an important role in determining the type and form of the test. Licensing tests are chosen by either the board or the administering agency from existing tests developed by the regulatory agency or through contract with a testing company or a consulting firm. Burns, Impara and Stoker, and Kane discuss the requirements of a licensing test. Burns closes his chapter with a series of questions that are helpful in making the choice of or developing a test.

Differences in the mode of pre-service training exist primarily in the relationship between training and test content. For some occupations, special pre-service training programs and workshops are designed from the content of the test to be given. (Coit and Cromack give an example of this process in real estate in Chapter Seven.) Workshops to prepare candidates for the certified public accounting license test and for state examinations in clinical psychology and law are frequently offered commercially. Practice in other occupations may demand more individual development and education than an occupation-specific training program. In these occupations training and education are provided through coursework and are offered through either higher education or vocational education institutions. In vocational education the training is frequently supplemented by an apprenticeship experience, cooperative work experience, or on-the-job training. In some of these cases, testing to provide information for the licensing decision is made part of the pre-service training. In other occupations sources of pre-service training include commercially marketed and packaged programs, and the licensing decision is made completely independent of the pre-service training mode. Chapter Two reviews the licensing test, requirements, and options.

For some occupations, residency, or a supervised apprenticeship, is required prior to entry. Residency information pertinent to licensing frequently includes descriptions of the practice and strengths and weaknesses of the candidate.

The third area of candidate consideration is character. Licensed practice in many occupations is subject to codes of ethics essential to public protection. Many incidents of malpractice can be traced to breakdowns in the character of practitioners rather than inadequacies in work skills or knowledge. Licensing information about candidate character must usually be gained through references and analyses of life histories. In those occupations where character is a licensing consideration, residencies or probationary practice experiences may be required. The criterion of "good character," however, is at present controversial.

Application and Application Control Procedures. The application process is designed by the board and is the communication link between the board and potential candidates for licensure. The application process usually involves publication of information on fees, applicant eligibility requirements, and information on testing procedures. Usually, application information is made available through related associations and organizations, through career and training programs, and through general public depositories of occupational information. Most application processes use a standardized form that includes questions to establish eligibility for application and procedures necessary to supply credentials: affidavits, transcripts, and public records.

The board develops application control procedures to create records for each applicant, to account for each, to check eligibility, and to maintain confidentiality of information. Several processes are involved in the control procedure: a review of each application, and communication if the application is incomplete; notification to eligible applicants of the next step, which may involve obtaining references, and certifications or transcripts if this is not part of the application, or informing the applicant of the examination schedule; the creation of an applicant portfolio or record; a verification of applicant information from external sources; and the creation of information routing for the review process.

Application control must include measures to preserve the confidentiality of candidate information and an accounting system to keep up with applications at each stage. In Chapter Seven Cromack and Coit discuss the receipt control procedure of a state licensing system. In their discussion they point out that the licensing system must be concerned with appropriate scheduling of licensing steps, including training and testing time and location.

Review Procedures. The applicant's portfolio includes character references, documentation of prior work experience, documentation of training, standardized test results of KSAs, performance appraisals on job-related exercises, interview summaries, evaluation of oral examinations, observations of supervised practice in the occupation, and ratings of work samples. For occupations where specific character concerns are not included in minimum standards and where licensing examination is directly linked to training for occupational entry, character references may be taken and reviewed at the time of entry into the training program. Otherwise, character references are collected for review during the application process. Documentation of prior work experience is also part of the application process. The candidate supplies this information with other pertinent data, including educational background. In occupations where character references and/or work experience are linked directly with minimum standards, the agency may independently query sources other than the applicant for this information.

Although there is a tendency to think of license granting as a simple process, the decision is actually a consideration of multivariate requirements. Although all qualifications are not reviewed at one time, each of the several requirements is reviewed at some point in the licensing process and serves to screen applicants at that stage. Hence, the process operates in the same manner as several sieves, with increasingly smaller meshes designed to sift and eliminate at each stage.

Regarding the compromises between public protection and candidates' rights, the licensing decision can be contrasted to a criminal court decision. In criminal court the defendant is assumed innocent until proven guilty. The assumption of innocence and burden of proof are designed so that the margin of error is in favor of protecting the individual. Hence, to convict an innocent man is considered a more serious error than freeing a guilty man. In the licensing decision, if there is public peril, which is the reason for regulation, there is a reversal of the direction of assumptions. In licensing, the candidate is assumed unqualified until sufficient evidence of qualification has been established. Hence, the admittance to practice of an unqualified candidate is deemed to be a more serious error than the rejection of a qualified candidate.

The board designs the notification procedures to be consistent with the rules, regulations, and policies. In the notification of each candidate, the information transmitted will differ depending on results of the licensure decision. If the candidate has been found qualified for licensing, the notification may inform the candidate of subsequent fees or of followup reporting requirements, or it may simply include the certification of license. Notice to the unsuccessful candidate will probably report to the candidate the areas in which she or he did not meet the standards; may inform the candidate of his or her rights for re-examination, reapplication, or a hearing; and will provide the candidate with an address for future correspondence. In Chapter Seven Cromack and Coit discuss how information obtained from meeting with unsuccessful candidates may be useful in the improvement of licensing tests.

Monitoring, Investigation, and Enforcement Procedures. Public protection through occupational licensing actually involves both regulation of entry and monitoring of practice. Shimberg (1980), in describing the useful function performed by regulatory boards, states that they perform the "screening [of] applicants to ensure that they possess at least the minimum qualifications for safe practice. Thus the public is spared the distress and practical hazard of dealing with unqualified practitioners. [other functions include] setting practice standards and codes of conduct for practitioners. These further safeguard the public, which often lacks a basis for judging what constitutes acceptable quality in service or conduct. . . . [They also serve in] investigating charges of incompetence or impropriety against licensees and taking appropriate disciplinary action where warranted. Such action not only helps to rid the profession of incompetent, unethical, and dishonest practitioners, but also serves notice on others that the regulatory agency will not tolerate practitioners when activities may be contrary to the public interest" (p. 6).

Due to limitations in resources, the primary mode of monitoring practitioners employed by regulatory boards is monitoring by exception—that is, the board receives complaints of substandard practice either from the public or from members of the occupational group, investigates each complaint, and prepares action according to its findings. Two other methods for monitoring inservice practice of regulated occupations are now under consideration by some regulatory agencies. The method which has received the most acceptance by members of regulated occupations is mandatory continuing education. Shimberg in Chapter One discusses the potential of this method for improving inservice practice of the occupation. In Chapter Six Bowering, Fortune, and Wood discuss periodic re-examination of licensees. Re-examination is another method for monitoring inservice practice, but due to opposition by occupational groups and logistical problems it has been implemented in only a few regulation systems.

The rules, regulations, and policies define provisions for enforcing regulation. This area in occupational licensing appears to be the weak link. Shimberg (1980) in discussing enforcement comments, "There is mounting evidence that while licensing boards have been very zealous about screening applicants to keep out incompetents, they have been somewhat lax in checking on those already licensed. Each year, boards receive thousands of complaints from various sources alleging incompetence, negligence, dishonesty, and unprofessional conduct on the part of licensees. Only a small fraction of these result in disciplinary action" (p. 101).

The weaknesses in enforcement can be attributed to several factors: The dependency on complaints allows some malpractice or incompetence to go undetected; weak laws allow repeated violations to go unpunished (Shimberg, 1980); and limited sanctions fail to meet the level of violation (Shimberg, 1980).

Establishment of System Requirements

In advancing an argument for application of the self-audit technique to improve practice, Shimberg (1980) identified ten areas in which questions should be asked about a licensing program: (1) need for continued regulation; (2) effectiveness; (3) rules, regulations, and policies; (4) license requirements; (5) reciprocity; (6) testing; (7) complaints and investigation; (8) enforcement; (9) public involvement; and (10) accountability. The questions for each area posed by Shimberg are listed in Table 3. Since the ten areas are focal points for self-evaluation of a licensing system, they also represent areas which should be investigated in reform or improvement efforts and which should be emphasized in the development or design of a new licensing system. These areas can be viewed as the basic system requirements of a licensing system, with the questions serving to indicate criteria for the satisfaction of each requirement.

Table 3. Suggested Self-Audit Questions for a Licensing Program

Area of Concern	*Questions*
Need for continued regulation	What problems and needs gave rise to regulation in the first place? Does this need for regulation still exist? In what ways would the absence of regulation endanger the public health, safety, or welfare?
Effectiveness	Has the board carried out its mission in an efficient, economic, and effective manner? Has the board compiled and disseminated a record of its accomplishment? How has the board's work provided positive benefits to the public?
Rules, regulations, and policies	Are board rules, regulations, and policies consistent with legislative intent? Do they clearly serve the public interest? Do the rules have the effect of restricting competition among practitioners? Can any board rules be interpreted as serving primarily the interests of the occupational group rather than those of the public?
License requirements	Can all requirements for licensure be justified as job-related and necessary to protect the public? Are some requirements too tough? Are some not tough enough? Has the board recommended constructive changes to the legislature?
Reciprocity	Do qualified out-of-state licensees have fair and reasonable access to the licensing process? With how many other states does the board have reciprocity agreements? How many out-of-state applicants does the board license via reciprocity? How many are turned down? For what reasons?
Testing	Are the tests used for licensure clearly related to those aspects of the job that involve protection of the public? Was a systematic job analysis conducted and were the findings documented, or was some other acceptable method used to establish job requirements? Is there a clear linkage between the job analysis and the test specifications? Do the tests meet professional measurement standards? What assurance is there that the answers labeled correct are not arbitrary? What assurance is provided that tests given at different times are comparable in their coverage and difficulty? Is there a rationale for the way in which passing scores are determined?
Complaints and investigation	Does the board wait for complaints to come in, or does it actively monitor the practices of its licensees through the use of investigators? What hap-

Table 3. Suggested Self-Audit Questions for a Licensing Program, Cont'd.

Area of Concern	*Questions*
	pens when complaints are received? Is any record made of the nature of the complaint and where it came from? Can the board show that it has considered and acted on all complaints? How many complaints are settled informally? Are records kept of informal settlements? Could such settlements be construed as a device by which the occupational group protects its members against disciplinary action? Can the board's resolution of complaints be translated into dollar savings or better service for consumers? If there is a recovery fund, how has it benefited consumers? To what extent have the investigatory efforts of the board been hampered by inadequate funding? What efforts, if any, has the board made to obtain additional funding?
Enforcement	How many complaints have gone to a formal hearing over the past three years? How many licenses were suspended or revoked? Does the board keep a record of reasons for taking disciplinary action? How many involved violations of rules designed to protect the consumer from fraud or deception? Can the board's enforcement activities be perceived as industry-oriented rather than consumer-oriented? Does the board feel that it has been handicapped in disciplining licensees because legal grounds for action are either too vague or too restrictive? If so, has the board sought the authority it needs to deal with the full range of disciplinary problems it faces?
Public involvement	Has the board sought to involve the public in its meetings and rule-making activities? Has the board established channels of communication with consumer groups to identify problems and develop solutions? What specifications has the board taken as a result of interchanges with consumer groups? Are there any public members on the board? If not, has the board advocated adding them?
Accountability	If the board is accountable to some higher authority in state government, how has it met its responsibility for keeping that authority informed of its activities? Has it prepared and disseminated in-

(continued on next page)

Table 3. Suggested Self-Audit Questions for a Licensing Program, Cont'd.

Area of Concern	*Questions*
	formative reports citing its accomplishments as well as actual or anticipated problems? Has it reported on issues that may involve conflicts between the interests of the public and those of an occupational group? Has it asked for additional resources or legislative authority to enable it to do its job more effectively?

Source: Adapted from Shimberg, 1980.

Importance of the Licensing Process

Licensure is authorization of actions regulated by law in order to protect public health and safety. Licensing protects public health and safety through either or both of two actions—regulation of entry into occupational practice and regulation of the level of quality of occupational practice. Accuracy in the licensing decision is important to the public, to the candidate, and to the regulatory agency itself.

In theory, the regulation of entry into practice protects the public by keeping incompetent or unqualified persons out of the occupation; guaranteeing a minimum level of knowledge, skills, and abilities of those entering the occupation; and improving through selection the beginning level of practice in the occupation. Ideally, regulation of the level of practice protects the public by monitoring, setting minimum-level standards of KSAs, recognizing and certifying levels of expertise or specialties, removing incompetents or unethical persons, and fostering periodic updating of required KSAs. The importance of licensure decisions is that they provide the confidence that practitioners are competent and ethical in areas which demand expertise beyond the layman's ability to recognize and to judge.

Licensing serves the candidate both directly and indirectly. Direct services of the licensing system to the candidate include a legal public record that the licensee is qualified, authorization to practice within the jurisdiction of the regulatory agency, and guidelines and standards for continued practice. Indirect benefits include limiting with entry standards the number of applicants, self-esteem gained from knowing that requirements are met, the prestige and trust rendered to practitioners in a regulated occupation, standardization of monitored practice, and elimination from practice of incompetent or unethical practitioners.

Licensing provides the regulatory agency with a legal vehicle through which standards can be influenced, authority to monitor entry and practice, means for protection of public health and safety, an avenue to influence training, a process to raise revenue serving to defray cost of regulation, and the rendering of correct determinations on applicants without the anticipation of protest or litigation.

Research into the Generic Process

Several research thrusts offer potential in licensing. Perhaps the most obvious is study of the process in regard to existing issues. For instance, study of consistency in requirements for licensing a specific occupation may shed light on the lack of reciprocity. Comparisons of monitoring methods may tend to validate or repudiate beliefs in continuing education requirements or re-examinations. Studies could be designed to investigate the utility of lay membership on licensing boards. Another research thrust could involve the evaluation of current types of systems. A simple but systematic application of the self-audit questions would provide potentially useful information on the operation of any licensing system. An additional approach might focus on variations of practice across licensing programs. The era of research into the generic process is just beginning.

References

Gagne, R. M. "Military Training and Principles of Learning." *American Psychologist,* 1962, *17,* 83-91.

Kronenberg, P. S., Rogers, B. D., and Greene, B. P. *Program Evaluation Methodology.* Knoxville, Tenn.: The Bureau of Public Administration, 1980.

Miller, R. B. "Analysis and Specification of Behavior for Training. In R. Glaser (Ed.), *Training Research and Education.* Pittsburgh, Penn.: University of Pittsburg, 1962.

Shimberg, B. *Occupational Licensing: A Public Perspective.* Princeton, N.J.: Educational Testing Service, 1980.

Shimberg, B., Esser, B. F., and Kruger, D. H. *Occupational Licensing: Practices and Policies.* Washington, D.C.: Public Affairs Press, 1972.

10

Developments and Trends in Licensing and Licensure Examinations

Robert L. Linn

Some 800 occupations are regulated by state governments (Greene and Gay, 1980; Shimberg, 1981). If local and federal regulations are considered, the number is even larger. Although not all regulations involve licensure, it is clear that regulation either in the form of practice control (licensing) or in the form of title control (certification) is pervasive (Shimberg, 1982).

Licensing boards have traditionally enjoyed considerable autonomy. Legislative mandates generally have left boards with a substantial degree of discretion in defining the operational requirements for licensure. Boards have been relatively free to establish specific requirements in the form of level and type of education, years of experience, character, and the type and level of performance on an examination. "Many of the requirements found in licensing statutes are there by dint of custom. They are seldom based on a careful analysis of the job to determine objectively what minimum level of knowledge, skill, ability, or other characteristics are necessary for practice in the given occupation" (Shimberg, 1982, p. 35).

There are a number of reasons to think that boards may be called upon to justify their procedures more frequently in the future. The public awareness of licensing and concern about regulation have increased in recent years. Approximately two thirds of the states have enacted some type of sunset legislation since the original sunset law was enacted in Colorado in 1976. As noted in Chapter One, sunset hearings have already led to reforms in some licensing procedures. They have also focused greater public attention on the process. Although judicial scrutiny of the use of tests by state agencies for licensing has been much less than that for employment tests, the threat of litigation is non-trivial and provides another stimulus for change. Hence, it seems appropriate to begin this chapter with a brief consideration of the types of evidence that boards may need to provide to justify their procedures. This discussion will be followed by consideration of possibilities for future types of examinations.

Validity

The foremost question regarding any testing program is that of validity. Although a new testing system may be preferred over an old one because of its greater efficiency, its lower cost, or its modern appearance, such characteristics are not substitutes for validity of the interpretations and uses of the test results.

Despite the central importance of validity, it is a topic that frequently seems to receive less attention in licensing and certification contexts than in many other testing contexts. Hecht (1979), for example, concluded in her review of the status of validating professional licensing and certification exams that "validation studies of licensure exams are rare indeed" (p. 21).

There are a number of reasons that test validation may be given insufficient attention in licensing and certification programs. To begin with, the problem of validation seems much more complicated for a licensure exam than for an employment test or a college admissions test, particularly if one takes the position espoused by some (for example, Hecht, 1979; Hogan, 1979; Menges, 1975; Pottinger, 1979) that licensure exams are best thought of as predictors of future performance and therefore "that predictive criterion-related validation studies would be the type most closely fitting the expressed purpose of licensure exams" (Hecht, 1979, p. 21). Furthermore, as was indicated in chapters Three and Four, there are important differences in opinion regarding the extent and types of evidence that are needed to support the validity of a licensure exam.

Criterion-related validation is never easy. Even when the focus is on a single job with considerable uniformity of tasks for a large number of incumbents, it is no simple matter to develop a justifiable criterion measure. In licensure testing the task is complicated manyfold by the fact that those who are licensed work in a wide range of job assignments for many different employers. Self-employment is also common in a number of occupations requiring licensure. As noted by Shimberg (1981, p. 1143), "a criterion-related validity study of a specific licensing or certification test may not be technically feasible."

More fundamental than the question of technical feasibility, however, is the question of the appropriateness of this approach to validation of a licensing exam. Kane (1982) has distinguished between two interpretations of scores on a licensing exam: as "predictors of future performance in practice" (pp. 917-918) and as "indicators of abilities that are critical for practice" (p. 918). The former interpretation calls for criterion-related validation. However, the latter interpretation, which Kane persuasively argued "provides a more modest and a more realistic standard for judging licensure examinations" (p. 918), calls for evidence of content and construct validity.

The primary rationale for licensing is "to protect the public health, safety, and welfare" (Shimberg, 1981, p. 1140). The goal of protecting the public from incompetent practitioners is quite different from an employer's goal of maximizing productivity. A skill that may be quite important to success on the job may be quite inappropriate for inclusion on a licensure exam. Shimberg (1981) illustrated the distinction between skills and abilities that are relevant to job success and those that are necessary to protect the public with the following example.

"Certain types of knowledge and skill that may be very important to job success might not be appropriate for inclusion on a licensing examination. For example, a pleasing personality and sales ability are usually considered important attributes for success as a real estate salesperson. Anyone developing a test to select personnel for this occupation would almost certainly strive to assess these qualities in some way. However, since the licensing agency is not concerned with predicting job success, it would probably ignore such attributes (even though they may be job-related) in favor of knowledge and skill directly related to the purpose of licensing, which is to protect the public'' (p. 1140).

Deciding what is appropriate to include on a licensure exam requires both logical analysis and empirical evidence. Job analyses can play a vital role in this process. However, it is essential that such analyses stress the criticality of the knowledge and skills for those aspects of the job that bear a logical relationship to the public's health, safety, and welfare. Frequency of occurrence is of less concern than criticality and the likelihood of harm due to lack of knowledge or the inability to perform. "Given that the purpose of licensure is to protect the public, the 'harmful if missed' category should be emphasized in licensure examinations'' (Kane, 1982, p. 916). A similar point is made in Chapter Three of this volume.

It is expected that boards will be called upon to defend the validity of their examinations more often in the future than was true in the past. Undoubtedly there are some who will not be satisfied without evidence of criterion-related validity. However, a strong case can be made that evidence of content and construct validity is both more feasible to obtain and more relevant to the purposes of licensing examinations. However, it should be emphasized that the latter types of evidence need to be accumulated in a much more systematic and rigorous fashion than is typical of previous practice.

Unsupported opinions of board members, despite their status and possibly clear expertise in the field, cannot be expected to suffice. Job analyses which show not only the frequency but also the criticality of the knowledge, skill, or ability for the intended purpose of the licensing will be needed.

Forms of Examinations

Although there are numerous examples of performance, essay, and oral examinations, "[t]he format most commonly used in licensing is the written multiple-choice test" (Shimberg, 1981, p. 1139). Multiple-choice tests are highly efficient and, when well developed, can be an effective means of measuring critical knowledge and abilities. However, they are apt to be most effective for measuring the more academic aspects of the occupation and, in some instances, may require more verbal skills than are necessary for competent practice. Some critics also object to the emphasis on discrete bits of knowledge found in some multiple-choice tests and argue that other approaches are needed to measure the complexities required in practice.

Performance tests often have considerable face validity and are used for a variety of occupations (such as aircraft mechanics, barbering, and dentistry). However, such tests are expensive to administer, frequently suffer from poor interrater reliability, and may be subject to charges of rater bias. As noted by Shimberg (1981, p. 1140), "ratings . . . can be influenced by considerations of sex, race, or other factors . . . because the examiners usually observe applicants directly when evaluating performance."

Simulations can sometimes provide a means of testing that approximates the reality of a performance test while maintaining much of the objectivity of a written multiple-choice test. Patient management problems used by the American Board of Medical Examiners provide an example of one of the better-known simulation tests. Test-takers are presented with a limited amount of information about a simulated patient. The test-taker can request additional information (for example, history, results of laboratory tests) until he or she is prepared to make a diagnosis and recommend treatment. Although scoring is considerably more complicated and subject to debate than the scoring of a multiple-choice test, it can, unlike most performance tests, be objectively specified and evaluated by other experts.

Most patient management problems have been presented in test booklets with the patient information and results of laboratory tests printed in invisible ink. When the test-taker marks a response area with a special felt-tip pen. the concealed information is made visible. In recent years, however, it has become increasingly common to use computers to administer patient management problems.

Computer-Administered Tests. The ready availability of relatively inexpensive computer technology opens many new possibilities for testing. Adaptive tests and simulation tests that are much too cumbersome to administer in a paper-and-pencil mode seem quite feasible on a computer. The possibilities are appealing. However, it must be recognized at the outset that it takes more than better tools to make better products.

GIGO, a familiar acronymn in computer jargon, stands for "garbage in, garbage out." Despite its seductiveness, sophisticated computer hardware provides no guarantee of improvements in testing. The validity of a multiple-choice test is no greater when it is scored by a high-speed optical scanner than when it is carefully scored by hand with the aid of an old-fashioned stencil. Neither will computerized test administration by itself enhance validity. Improvements in validity will depend on the quality of the content and on the nature of the test exercises that are created for computer administration.

Three applications of computers as testing devices that are expected to become increasingly familiar in the future are described in the following sections. The first, adaptive tests, can be developed with traditional test items of either the multiple-choice or free-response variety. The potential advantage of such tests is derived from their sequential use of information. Following each response to a test item, the computer calculates an estimate of the test-taker's ability and either selects another item that will yield the maximum additional information or terminates the test with a score that satisfies pre-specified characteristics.

The second application, simulation tests, represents a sharper departure from traditional paper-and-pencil tests. Although there are a number of well-known examples, such as the tab-item test (Glaser, Damrin, and Gardner, 1954), the in-basket test (Frederiksen, Jenson, and Beaton, 1972), and the previously mentioned patient management problem (McGuire, Solomon and Bashook, 1976) of non-computerized simulation tests, the computer has the potential for making such tests less cumbersome and more realistic.

The third application, self-assessment tests, could take a variety of forms including either adaptive tests or simulated problem-solving exercises. Of course, the computer is not a necessary device for all self-assessment tests. But, given ready availability, the computer could have several advantages for such tests, not the least of which is personal appeal to the test-taker. Other advantages might include scoring efficiency, ease of record keeping, opportunities to take multiple versions of the test, and the provision of diagnostic information and suggestions for remediating deficiencies.

Adaptive Tests. Adaptive tests, also known as tailored tests, branched tests, sequential tests, and response-contingent tests, have attracted considerable attention in the past ten or fifteen years. The military services currently have underway a major research and development program aimed at the introduction of an operational computerized adaptive testing system for their primary selection and classification testing.

Lord (1980) summarized the basic rationale for adaptive testing: "An examinee is measured most effectively when the test items are neither too difficult nor too easy for him. Thus for any given psychological trait the computer's main task at each step of the test administration might be to estimate tentatively the examinee's level on the trait, on the basis of his responses to whatever items have already been administered. The computer could then choose the next item to be administered on the basis of this tentative estimate." (p. 150)

Although some earlier attempts were based on notions from classical test theory, present approaches to adaptive tests rely on item response theory. Much of the theoretical foundation for adaptive testing was initially presented by Lord (1970). For more recent presentations of the theory see Hulin, Drasgow and Parsons (1983) and Lord (1980). Most of the theoretical and applied work has focused on tests that yield maximum information over a broad range of ability. Tentative ability estimates are obtained following each response to an item. The next item is selected such that it will yield the maximum information for a person with ability equal to the current tentative estimate. This typically means that a correct response will lead to the administration of a more difficult item and an incorrect response will lead to the administration of an easier item.

After each response the standard error of the tentative

ability estimate is also obtained. When the standard error falls below a pre-specified value or a maximum number of items have been administered, the testing is terminated and the latest estimate of ability is reported.

Adaptive tests of the type just described have several potential advantages over conventional paper-and-pencil tests: (1) They can yield considerably more accurate estimates at the extreme of the ability continuum. (2) For most examinees they can determine a given level of accuracy with fewer items. (3) They can virtually eliminate most problems of test compromise and cheating since each test-taker is administered a unique exam. (4) They make it possible to administer secure tests on demand rather than only on a few test administration dates each year.

Although the advantages of adaptive testing could be of considerable value for some licensing exams, the approach relies upon some strong theoretical assumptions and requires a great deal of prior information about the characteristics of a large pool of test items. Finally, better measurement at the extremes is of less importance for a licensing test than the accuracy of measurement near the minimum passing score. The most problematic assumption for some licensing tests is apt to be that of unidimensionality. This assumption is necessary for current applications of item response theory, but it would not be reasonable for a licensing test that was designed to measure several dimensions of professional competence. One possible solution to these problems would be to divide the item pool into relative homogeneous subsets and construct adaptive tests for each. Decision rules for licensing could then be based on the multiple scores produced by the separate adaptive tests.

The need for previously calibrated items may be a serious obstacle to adaptive testing, especially for relatively low-volume programs. Adequate estimates of item parameters for use in adaptive testing require sample sizes of roughly a thousand or more examinees. Even with efficient on-line calibration techniques, only programs with large numbers of candidates would be able to accumulate enough item response data to support an adaptive testing system.

The third drawback, that of a mismatch between the goal of the most valid and reliable dichotomous decision for a licensing test and the improved accuracy of measurement at the extremes provided by the usual adaptive testing strategy, suggests the need for an alternate adaptive strategy. Although there may be an interest in knowing how far a test-taker is above or below the minimum passing score, the primary concern is with the pass-fail decision. For this purpose, an adaptive test need not provide accurate discrimination among examinees at either extreme, but it should minimize the errors of classification.

Linn, Rock, and Cleary (1972) demonstrated that substantial savings in average testing time can be achieved using a simple sequential testing procedure. After the administration of each item a decision was made to fail, to pass, or to administer another item to the test-taker. A conventional test was shown to require approximately twice as many items on the average to achieve the same level of accuracy as the sequential testing procedure. This savings was accomplished using only conventional item difficulties and a prearranged item sequence that was far from optimal for the purpose. Considerably greater savings could be anticipated using more sophisticated procedures such as those described by Green (1970) and in Lord's (1980) discussion of mastery testing.

Simulation. The tab-item test developed by Glaser, Damrin, and Gardner (1954) has considerable appeal for many occupations where diagnostic problem solving is a critical feature of the job. Problems faced in television repair were simulated. A symptom—for example, no picture on the screen—was presented followed by a list of possible actions—turn up the brightness and contrast controls, check the video amplifer outlet with an oscilloscope. The examinee selected actions to be taken in a sequential fashion and obtained the information resulting from the action by lifting a tab. For example, the wave form that would appear on an oscilloscope when the video amplifer outlet was checked was printed under a tab.

The tab-item test was an important innovation. But due to the mode of presentation, it was static in character. That is, the decision to perform one check did not alter the results that would be obtained in performing another check. It was not possible, for example, to replace a part and then get altered results from appropriate checks performed subsequently. More importantly, the tab-item technology was rather cumbersome to construct, reproduce, and score. These drawbacks probably contributed to the limited amount of use that has been made of the technique. However, the basic concept of the tab-item test is sound, and the technological limitations can be easily overcome on a computer.

Patient management problems are intended to simulate a clinical problem, a physician's encounter with a patient. McGuire and Babbott (1967) identified six essential characteristics of a good simulation of a clinical problem.

> A clinical problem which purports to simulate the physician-patient encounter must have the following characteristics: First, it must be initiated by information of the type a patient gives a physician, not by a predigested summary of the salient features of the case, and if it is to be realistic it must be couched in terms the patient or a referring physician would use. Second, the exercise must require a series of sequential, interdependent decisions representing the various stages in the diagnostic work-up and management of the patient. Third, the examinee must be able to obtain in realistic form information about the results of each decision, as a basis for subsequent action. Fourth, once these data are obtained it must be impossible for the examinee to retract a decision that is revealed to be ineffectual or harmful. Fifth, the problem must be constructed so as to allow both for different medical approaches and for variation in patient responses appropriate to these several approaches. Hence, provision must be made for modifications in the problem as the patient responds to the specific interventions chosen by each examinee. Finally, these modifications must differ among examinees, according to the unique configuration of prior decisions each has made (pp. 1–2).

The characteristics listed by McGuire and Babbott distinguish the clinical simulation from other problem-solving simulations such as the tab-item test. The desirability of dynamic rather than static problems is not limited to clinical problems of physicians. Many important problems encountered in occupations requiring licensure are dynamic in character. Preliminary actions affect the results of subsequent actions. Simulations of practical problems which ignore the interactive character of the problem may miss a crucial aspect of competent practice. Interactive adaptation of a test "according to the unique configuration of prior decisions" of each examinee requires individualization of the kind that can best be achieved by a computer.

Self-Assessment. Self-assessment can be of value to the person preparing to take a licensing test for the first time as well as to the licensed practitioner. For the practitioner, the results of self-assessment can identify areas where one is out of date and provide references for self-study or guidance in making choices regarding continuing education opportunities. "Perhaps the greatest value of self-assessment is the diagnostic feedback such programs provide" (Shimberg, 1982, p. 132).

A number of self-assessment programs are currently available, most commonly in health-related occupations. As the name implies, the results of self-assessment tests are private. A central agency may keep group statistics that are useful in judging the general level of knowledge of practitioners, but individual results are not reported to third parties.

Mandatory re-examination for relicensure is often proposed, but there is little indication that the field is moving in that direction. On the other hand, mandatory continuing education has become increasingly common in the past decade. Self-assessment tests can provide a needed diagnostic tool for sensible selection among continuing education options.

Predictions for the Future of Licensing

Predictions about the future are always hazardous. Complex systems develop in very unpredictable ways and are subject to social and political influences that are poorly understood. Licensing is largely a creature of legislative action and therefore subject to all the vagaries of this process. Nonetheless, two predictions have been made. First, boards can expect that they will be more likely to be called upon to justify their procedures in the future than was true in the past. Evidence of the validity of examinations for determining whether a candidate has the necessary knowledge, skills, and abilities for competent practice will be crucial in justifying the licensing process. Second, computer technology will alter the form of many licensing examinations. Greater efficiency due to adaptive sequential test administration will be achieved. Greater fidelity of the problem-solving tasks that are crucial in many occupations will be achieved with the use of computerized problem simulations.

References

Frederiksen, N., Jenson, O., and Beaton, A. E. *Prediction of Organizational Behavior.* Elmsford, N.Y.: Pergamon Press, 1972.

Glaser, R., Damrin, D. E., and Gardner, E. M. *The Tab Item: A Technique for the Measurement of Proficiency in Diagnostic Problem-Solving Tasks.* Urbana, Ill.: University of Illinois, College of Education, Bureau of Research and Service, 1954.

Green, B. F., Jr. "Comments on Tailored Testing." In W. H. Holtzman (Ed.), *Computer-Assisted Instruction, Testing, and Guidance.* New York: Harper & Row, 1970.

Greene, K., and Gay, R. *Occupational Regulation in the United States.* Washington, D.C.: U.S. Department of Labor, Employment and Training Administration, 1980.

Hecht, K. A. "Current Status and Methodological Problems of Validating Professional Licensing and Certification Exams." In M. A. Bunda and J. R. Sanders (Eds.), *Practices and Problems in Competency-Based Education.* Washington, D.C.: National Council on Measurement in Education, 1979.

Hogan, D. *The Regulation of Psychotherapists.* Vol. 11: *A Study in the Philosophy and Practice of Professional Regulation.* Cambridge, Mass.: Ballinger, 1979.

Hulin, C. L., Drasgow, F., and Parsons, C. K. *Item Response Theory: Application to Psychological Measurement.* Homewood, Ill.: Dow Jones-Irwin, 1983.

Kane, M. T. The Validity of Licensure Examinations. *American Psychologist,* 1982, *37,* 911-918.

Linn, R. L., Rock, D. A., and Cleary, T. A. "Sequential Testing for Dichotomous Decisions." *Educational and Psychological Measurement,* 1972, *32,* 85-95.

Lord, F. M. "Some Test Theory for Tailored Testing." In W. H. Holtzman (Ed.), *Computer-Assisted Instruction, Testing, and Guidance.* New York: Harper & Row, 1970.

Lord, F. M. *Applications of Item Response Theory to Practical Testing Problems.* Hillsdale, N.J.: Erlbaum, 1980.

McGuire, C. H., and Babbott, D. "Simulation Techniques in the Measurement of Problem Solving." *Journal of Educational Measurement,* 1967, *4,* 1-10.

McGuire, C., Solomon, L., and Bashook, P. *Construction and Use of Written Simulations.* New York: Psychological Corporation, 1976.

Menges, R. J. "Assessing Readiness for Professional Practice." *Review of Educational Research,* 1975, *45,* 172-203.

Pottinger, P. S. "Competence Testing as a Basis for Licensing: Problems and Prospects." In M. A. Bunda and J. R. Sanders (Eds.), *Practices and Problems in Competency-Based Education.* Washington, D.C.: National Council on Measurement in Education, 1979.

Shimberg, B. "Testing for Licensure and Certification." *American Psychologist,* 1981, *36,* 1138-1146.

Shimberg, B. *Occupational Licensing: A Public Perspective.* Princeton, N.J.: Educational Testing Service, 1982.

Index